W9-BNK-244

ACCOMPANYING THE JOURNEY:

A Handbook for Sponsors

BY
LESTER RUTH

DISCIPLESHIP RESOURCES

P.O. BOX 840 • NASHVILLE, TENNESSEE 37202-0840

Scripture quotations, unless otherwise indicated, are from the New Revised Standard Version of the Bible, copyright © 1989 by the Division of Christian Education of the National Council of Churches of Christ in the USA.

Library of Congress Catalog Card No. 96-86587

ISBN 0-88177-176-7

ACCOMPANYING THE JOURNEY: A Handbook for Sponsors. Copyright © 1997 Discipleship Resources. All rights reserved. No part of this book may be reproduced in any form whatsoever, print or electronic, without written permission from the publisher, except in the case of brief quotations embodied in critical articles or reviews. For more information contact Discipleship Resources Editorial Offices, P.O. Box 840, Nashville, Tennessee 37202-0840.

DR176

CONTENTS

PREFACE

I learned long ago that a project like this is really a cooperative effort. Although only one set of hands hit the keyboard, many have contributed to the final product.

First, I would like to thank Daniel Benedict and the others at the General Board of Discipleship whose dreams inspired this series in general and this volume in particular. Many thanks, too, to those who have offered helpful comments during my writing, particularly Grant Sperry-White and Karen Westerfield Tucker. I also thank David Brown, who gave me wise counsel during the time I wrote. Much gratitude is extended also to First United Methodist Church in Overton, Texas, for its prayers and patience with its pastor during this process. In the same regard I thank my wife, Carmen Ruth, for her undaunted encouragement and support. I also wish to thank my "safety net," Beth Boardman, who continues to make so many fine comments to improve my writing. I send a special note of love to my father, Charles K. Ruth, who has made so many things possible for me. Finally, I wish to thank all the sponsors—particularly Donna Edwards—at the churches I have served. Their dedication has been the true inspiration behind this book. To them, I dedicate this resource.

INTRODUCTION

John Wesley, one of the originators of Methodism, once said, "Christianity is essentially a social religion;...to turn it into a solitary religion is indeed to destroy it."[1] By this statement, Wesley highlighted the critical communal nature of true Christianity: Christians need each other; we cannot go it alone.

This book honors the essentially social nature of Christianity by discussing how faith formation happens in the process of Christian initiation. Simply put, as Christians, we grow best when we have others to help us along the journey.

This idea will be repeated many times as it is presented among the specific topics of this book: the ministries of Christians, called sponsors, who assist in the formation of those preparing for baptism, those preparing for the baptism of their children, or those preparing to reaffirm the covenant explicit in baptism. This book explores how sponsors best fulfill the social principle of Christianity in their important ministry. As the title suggests, sponsors are committed Christians who accompany people in this preparation and in their subsequent Christian walk.

As sponsors read this book, they should realize that their ministry is a venerable and ancient one, reaching back to the earliest centuries of the Christian church. Although a detailed historical examination occurs only in Chapter Six, this book is indebted and committed to the classic form of sponsorship used in the early church.

Significantly, the art of sponsorship practiced by early Christians is being revived and appropriated by several denominations in our day. The early church (and a growing number of present-day churches) viewed baptism as part of a process in which adults to be baptized were progressively formed in the faith as they engaged in a variety of ministries. The early church called this process of formation and instruction in preparation for baptism a *catechumenate*. Sponsors played (and continue to play) an especially important role when they accompany their initiates, or charges, in preparation for baptism—the heart of the process of Christian initiation. (In this book the terms "initiate" and "charge" are used interchangeably to refer to anyone for whom sponsors have responsibility throughout the initiation process; the term "candidate" is used only for people preparing for baptism during the intensive preparation stage.)

As is the case with the other volumes in the Christian Initiation series, the primary focus of this handbook is the process of accompanying the *adult seeker* to the waters of baptism. However, since the needs of congregations vary, two adaptations to the process—for the initiation of children and for baptized seekers—are treated in some detail in Chapters One and Two. We invite church leaders, including sponsors, to use skill and creativity in adapting the material in this handbook to fit the sponsorial needs of their congregations. (See *Come to the Waters*, pp. 67-68 for more detail.)

This volume is intended as a practical handbook for sponsors. It supplements the other volumes in the Christian Initiation series. If this book does its job, it will help sponsors develop a hands-on approach to guide those being initiated. It will also help sponsors understand their ministry.

It is hoped that the organization of this book will contribute toward fulfilling both tasks. The first chapter outlines the basic goals and duties of a sponsor's ministry and sketches an understanding of baptism that links it with intentional formation in the faith. The next three chapters discuss the details of a sponsor's ministry. Chapter Two covers the worship role of sponsors. Chapters Three and Four outline a sponsor's ministry outside of worship. Again, in all three chapters, the thread that ties it all together is the notion of *presentation*.

The book concludes with two auxiliary chapters. Chapter Five discusses a wide range of practical issues for sponsors and also provides an annotated reading list. Chapter Six provides a concise history of the ministry of sponsors. The Appendix contains a brief order for the commissioning of sponsors. This service is very important since it allows sponsors and the congregation to publicly affirm their mutual responsibility and support for the process of Christian initiation.

As I wrote this book, I was struck by the potential difficulty in trying to create a practical guide that would be useful in a denomination like The United Methodist Church. The difficulty comes from the diversity we have as a church: great theological, racial, and cultural breadth, among others. I invite—no, I beg—you, the reader, to make any and all adaptations of my suggestions to fit your particular circumstances. My fervent prayer is that this volume will be helpful somehow in bringing people to a deeper relationship with Christ.

—Lester Ruth

UNDERSTANDING THE TASK OF A SPONSOR

WHAT IS A SPONSOR?

Suppose your family is holding an open house. The housecleaning is complete. The refreshments are meticulously prepared. Much effort has gone into making your home an inviting, friendly place. You want your guests to be awed by your hospitality. Will they want to come inside and partake?

Now, imagine this is an exceptional sort of open house. Its purpose is to entice the guests to become part of your family and members of the household. Your family is close-knit, bonded to each other by common love, common commitment, and common experiences. This unity itself presents a quandary. Simultaneously, it is attractive to the non-family member because of the love and familiarity, and yet it is somewhat intimidating because the nonmember recognizes that she or he is not yet part of the family circle. Who can help the guests bridge this gap between attraction and intimidation?

If you have been called to be a sponsor in the process of Christian initiation, you can and you should be able to bridge this gap. The open house example parallels a church trying to initiate new members. The qualities that make a church and Christianity attractive are often the same qualities that intimidate potential members. Someone is needed to convey the church's hospitality and desire for potential members and new members. Someone is needed to show new members, once they are inside the house, how to maneuver around their new home, to get to know its nooks and crannies, to get to know all the "insider" information. Someone is needed to introduce new members to the other members of the household. That someone is a sponsor.

Your role as a sponsor will be described in this book through a variety of images. Many of them will revolve around one central notion: *presentation*. Put simply, a sponsor is a presenter. A sponsor presents the church and the gospel of Jesus Christ to the new member, and introduces this person to the church. The sponsor is the point of contact between the one being initiated and the church. The introductions and presentations must go in both directions.

A sponsor makes several kinds of presentations on behalf of the "household" to the "guest." One is the initial invitation. How will others know the good news about the feast unless someone extends the invitation? And, to follow that, how many guests will stay if no one greets and welcomes them? It is difficult to approach and remain in a new place and group on one's own. It is much easier if someone from the household is ready to greet the newcomer at the first approach. Someone must attend to the needs, questions, and desires of the guest. Someone must offer the home's abundance of hospitality so that the guest acquires the familiarity to truly become a member.

And who better to present the guest to the household than the sponsor? A sponsor presents the newcomer to the church the same way as she or he would at an open house. The sponsor names the newcomer, stands with her or him and escorts the initiate—sometimes literally—through the dimensions of the church household that have long become familiar and meaningful to those who already belong.

In more explicitly theological language, the sponsor presents to the initiate the church, its way of life, and the gospel it preaches. The sponsor makes specific and concrete the attitude of the church, and, through the church, the ultimately gracious welcome of God. In other words, the sponsor represents (re-*presents*) to each newcomer the Christian attitudes that the church holds for its new members: welcome, concern, support, love, and accountability. An initiate should see these things in her or his sponsor.

A sponsor stays with an initiate throughout the entire process. The church, as will be discussed later, may also call upon a sponsor to verify the newcomer's readiness to be received into the church. This is presentation by confirmation: By confirming the initiate's readiness, a sponsor formally presents her or him to the congregation.

However, the responsibility for assisting the newcomer does not belong solely to the sponsor. This important task belongs to the whole church foremost and then to particular individuals. A sponsor is part of this team of ministers.

Included in this team, of course, is the pastor of the church, whose primary role is to "receive and articulate the vision of welcoming seekers and making disciples."[2] In other words, a pastor brings zeal—the "umph"—to the task of initiating and making new disciples for Christ. The pastor holds important oversight responsibilities for the whole initiation process and plays special roles within the worship services themselves.

Another crucial leader is the catechist (also called a formation director). Compared to a sponsor, a catechist has a more directly instructional role for a church newcomer. Catechists lead "formational group sessions" in which initiates are formed as Christians. Catechists present God's Word to initiates to help them become Scripture-based Christians in thoughts, beliefs, words, and actions. To stay informed about this crucial dimension of their initiates' faith formation, sponsors should attend all formational group sessions with their initiates. (More information on the ministry of the catechist can be found in *Echoing the Word: The Ministry of Forming Disciples*, published by Discipleship Resources.)

Depending on the size of the church and the number of initiates at any one time, a church may have one or more of the following initiation ministries:

- an initiation coordinator
- one or more hospitality directors—responsible for initiates' immediate physical

needs, such as childcare, transportation, towels, and baptismal garments. (In no way should the existence of such a position relieve a sponsor from her or his primary responsibility of expressing the church's hospitality.)

• a specially appointed worship director and musicians

What makes a sponsor's role distinct from these other ministries? Probably the level of specific concern for the initiate. Everyone involved hopes that the newcomer finds the church hospitable and learns the Christian way. But the sponsor works further to make sure the initiate receives individual care. That is the amazing thing about God's grace: Freely directed to all people, it is given to each as if the individual involved is the only object of God's love. By personal, individual attachment and attention, a sponsor helps an initiate experience this fact.

HOW LONG DOES A BAPTISM TAKE?

At first glance the above question seems simple enough: It takes only a moment to apply water—usually a small sprinkle at that—to a person and pronounce her or him baptized in the name of the Triune God. It appears to be a silly question.

But is it really? What if we considered that baptism included the acceptance of and the ability to live out a wide range of Christian beliefs and attitudes? What if baptism were defined to include someone's conversion and subsequent willingness to live as a fruitful member of the church? What if baptism were understood as a *process* through which a person becomes fully immersed in Christ, in the reign of God, and in the church? Understood in that way, baptism would definitely take more time than a few passing moments—much more time.

It is this understanding of baptism that is advocated in this handbook and its companion volumes in the Christian Initiation series. Because the purpose of the instruction is to form the initiate as a Christian in every dimension of life, it is perhaps best to see initiation as a process taking place over a period of time. Making pottery from clay demands a gradual process of shaping, molding, and adjusting—even if God is the potter!

To say that baptism or initiation requires time is not to deny an instantaneous nature for conversion or commitment in some people. But dramatic experiences have a context; they are part of a larger spiritual journey. Some contact with Christians and the gospel usually precedes such an experience; some participation in the church and acceptance of the gospel should follow. The emphasis should be on this broader context, rather than the experience itself. The church may justifiably ask for a period of formation between initial happenings and the time of full initiation. Indeed, the description of baptism, initiation, and the role of the sponsor in this handbook and in its companion volumes assumes this understanding.

Throughout the church's history, vivid images have been used to highlight the progressive but gradual nature of initiation.[3] Preparation for baptism has been likened to the forty-year wilderness journey of the children of Israel. Time passed between the escape from Egypt and the arrival in the Promised Land. The military provides another image. A soldier is not sent to the battlefield immediately after being recruited or drafted. Instead, the recruit is sent to boot camp to be trained for the task that lies ahead. A final image compares being baptized to the process of human conception, growth in the womb, and birth. Babies are not immediately born after having been conceived. Rather a process of growth in a secure, nurturing environment takes place until the time for birth. The process and activities surrounding the inquiring newcomer to the church are exactly that: a secure, nurturing environment provided by the church until the moment of baptism and, beyond baptism, until the new member has been fully integrated into the life of the congregation.

Returning to the analogy of the church as an open house, one can say that the porch of a house gives the guest a place to comfortably prepare for entry. For a church to provide a newcomer time for Christian formation, structures to encourage formation, and leaders (sponsors, catechists, and pastors) to assist in formation, is to offer an entryway, or "porch." *Come to the Waters* aptly describes the initiation process in this way:

> People who are searching for God need more than abruptly ascending steps that usher them directly into the house. They are not ready for that. Steps that lead to an open space where they can test, explore, search, and experience God's welcome in the faith community, are analogous to a porch. Porches are gracious spaces between the steps and the house. On a porch, the people who live inside and the people who are approaching can meet, begin to know one another, and experience the climate of the house....On a porch, the congregation can extend the invitation to come inside when it senses that what has been shared on the porch recommends this invitation. Likewise, the seeker can evaluate and discern whether he or she has an interest in fuller participation in the life of the household of faith. A porch is an in-between place for people who are seeking God.[4]

A sponsor is one of the active, intentional hosts on the porch, extending the graciousness of the household in this in-between place and directing the attention of the seeker to the feast inside. An extended period of inquiry, formation, and intensive preparation takes place before the newcomer is finally ushered into the household through baptism.

The depth of the formation expected for initiation into the church—and, indeed, the call for a time of formation—is suggested by the baptismal service itself. In the part of the service called the "Renunciation of Sin and Profession of Faith," candidates who can answer for themselves and parents of children to be baptized make the following commitments: renunciation of the spiritual forces of wickedness; rejection of the evil powers of this world; repentance from sin; resistance of evil, injustice, and oppression; confession of Jesus Christ as Savior; a placing of one's whole trust in his grace; and a promise to serve Christ as Lord. What weightier, more solemn commitments could ever be made? The goal, as stated in the congregation's pledge of commitment, is that those initiated may be true disciples "who walk in the way that leads to life."[5]

All this language confirms that initiation is a progressive journey over time. If a true disciple is one who *walks*, then a journey with Christ is apparent. And it is a walk in *a way*. The goal of initiation is for the initiate to acquire:

- a *way* of knowing God, not just recalling memorized information.
- a *way* of life with God, not just adapting to certain rules of behavior.
- a *way* of believing and trusting in a gracious God, not just reciting specific beliefs.

The formation by sponsors and catechists may include these more elementary points, but it does not end there. The goal is nothing less than the formation of Christians equipped to walk in the way of eternal life while living in the modern world. Such formation takes time. Baptism, in this sense of the word, is a lifelong journey.

To understand baptism or initiation as a process over time, one can imagine Christianity as a language and Christian formation as learning to speak the language. As a "language," Christianity has a vocabulary: There are distinctive terms and phrases the church uses. The vocabulary also includes unique activities that serve as basic building blocks for speaking "Christian": prayer, worship, study, service, giving. And there is a grammar to Christianity. All of these vocabulary building blocks usually follow a set of rules for relating to one another. Longtime church members typically have learned how Christian essentials fit together. But it is not nearly as obvious to the newcomer. She or he must work hard on the vocabulary and grammar to gain the ability to speak fluent "Christian." This fluency is acquired over time by attending the "classroom" of worship services led by pastors, by participation in the "language labs" of formational group sessions led by catechists, and by working with sponsors who provide immediate opportunities to try out this new "language" and who should insist that the initiate try to "speak Christian" as much as possible. Like a language, Christianity is not learned until one uses it over and over.

This understanding of how one becomes a Christian should be natural for United Methodists; it is part of our early heritage. One early Methodist, Ebenezer Newell, while a seeker after faith and while observing Methodist worship, reported that he received divine instruction to "join the church."[6] Newell resisted, thinking that he was not fit to join. A question came to him: "Where would you go to learn the French language?" Newell replied that he would go live with the French. Another question came to him: "Where would you go then in order to learn the language of Canaan and the doctrines of Christ?" Newell finally realized that he should formally associate with the church and learn this "language." For early Methodists, this association would have meant participation in a small group called a "class meeting," where one learned to be a Christian, and in a variety of Methodist worship services.

Early Methodists, thus, understood being a Christian as a learned "art." They would have agreed with the assessment of one scholar who has described the goal of the initiation process as the "intricate art of gospel-living" acquired by apprenticeship to "master" Christians.[7] Or, as another expert put it: "One learns how to fast, pray, repent, celebrate, and serve the good of one's neighbor less by being lectured on these matters than by close association with people who do these things with regular ease and flair."[8] Not surprisingly, John Wesley, the founder of Methodism, once used a term from the early church, derived from this sort of initiation process and understanding of learning Christianity, to describe the most basic elements of early Methodist organization. Wesley argued that his organizing people as Methodists into societies (the original Methodist term for a group of Methodists in one locale) was nothing more than the early church had done in separating catechumens (the early church term for people preparing for baptism) for Christian formation.[9] Wesley and other early Methodists understood, just as the early church did, that time, a nurturing environment, and the assistance of mature Christians were the crucial components in forming newcomers in the Christian faith.

Not only does the nature of Christian formation need an extended time but also the contemporary situation makes intentional formation necessary. As Daniel T. Benedict Jr. discusses in *Come to the Waters,* we can no longer assume that North American society is forming people in the Christian tradition.[10] In a bold move, Benedict suggests that North America should be seen as a "mission frontier," where significant numbers of adults have not been baptized or have not had much experience with Christian churches. In such a case a congregation must be intentional in how it prepares its newcomers for initiation and Christian living. In a missionary setting churches must be aware of their own Christian distinctiveness and conscious about forming newcomers in it.

HOW THE PROCESS OF INITIATION WORKS

A sponsor assisting an initiate needs a thorough understanding of how the whole process fits together. A guide, which is what a sponsor is, needs a good sense of direction and a familiarity with the territory to lead others.

A newcomer moves through four basic stages during the initiation process: inquiry, formation, intensive preparation, and full integration into the life and ministry of the church. Returning to the image of the church as an open house, one can view each stage as a key element in moving from outside the house to inside. Inquiry, then, is the front steps. The period of formation is the front porch. The period of intensive preparation is the final step from the porch into the doorway of the house. Integration is being inside the house itself. (These stages will be discussed later in more detail.)

Movement between stages is marked by special worship services that serve as thresholds to the next stage. Between inquiry and the formation period, there is a service that welcomes the seekers and formally establishes them as "hearers." Between the formation period and the time of intensive preparation, there is a service that designates the hearers as candidates for initiation through baptism. After this period of intensive preparation, there follows the service of baptism itself. It is important not to think of baptism as just "one more step" in an ongoing process. Baptism represents both the heart and the culminating point of the whole process of initiation. With baptism the person finally walks through the door and becomes a member of Christ's household of faith. One may even say that every word spoken and every action taken in the initiation process thus far have served to prepare the candidate for the joyous event of baptism. But baptism is not a graduation that terminates the formation process. Following the example of the early church, formation continues, especially in the first weeks after initiation. As *Come to the Waters* suggests, this final formal period may climax with a service that affirms the new member's integration into the church and into her or his specific share in the ministry of the whole church. (Some adaptation of the process is necessary in the case of returning members, as will be shown later.)

Notice that in this way a regular rhythm is established in the initiation process between formation that occurs outside a worship setting and one that occurs within. This rhythm is helpful for the initiate, the church, and you, the sponsor. Having services that mark the thresholds can serve as reminders to all that the goal is progress in the Christian journey. For the initiate, the services serve as personal incentives to grow in grace and to continually move forward. They also help keep initiates fresh in the memory of the church. The services tend to awaken church members' sensibilities to the importance of introducing people to God's grace and to awaken their own initiation into this grace. For the sponsor, knowing what will be expected of you and your initiate in an upcoming worship service provides the basic framework for your work preceding that service.

Many congregations choose to correlate this rhythm with the church calendar of holidays. The connection is natural and historic, and it is usually strongest as the process nears the moment of initiation. While the service that welcomes the inquirer as a hearer may be conducted at any time, the service that marks the onset of intensive preparation (at which time the hearer becomes a candidate) usually occurs at the beginning of a traditional preparation period in the church year, preferably Lent or Advent. In this way, baptism or another initiation service can fall on or around one of the great holidays in the Christian Year: at the Easter Vigil or on Easter Day (when the intensive preparation occurred in Lent) or on the Baptism of the Lord (when the intensive preparation occurred during the weeks of Advent and Christmas). Finally, the service for affirming the ministry of the newly baptized or of returning members can occur at the holiday that marks the culmination of the previous church season. If the period of intensive preparation took place during Lent and initiation happened at Easter (this is the recommended scenario), the service of affirmation would occur on the Day of Pentecost. Alternatively, if the Advent-Christmas cycle was followed, the service of affirmation could occur on Transfiguration Sunday. *Come to the Waters* (pp. 71-85) provides a much fuller discussion of how to connect the initiation process with the church calendar.

Let us look at how this rhythm works in a variety of situations. One particularly important scenario is that of an adult who has never been baptized, the primary subject of this handbook and its companion volumes. The whole initiation process begins with a stage we call "inquiry" (see Figure 1, p. 14) from the viewpoint of the newcomer and "evangelization" from the viewpoint of the congregation. Since it is the initial stage, the church may make contact with the newcomer—now called an "inquirer"—in a variety of ways. The congregation should be careful to provide gentleness, sensitivity, and other basic elements of hospitality. The purpose of this stage is to assist the inquirer in clarifying her or his desires and motivations. This stage incorporates discussion about the most basic religious questions and motivations to help the inquirer discern an answer to the question, "What are you seeking?" Churches should connect a sponsor with an inquirer even at this early stage so that the church's care and help will be individual and specific.

Figure 1

The Rhythm of Stages and Services for Adults Seeking Baptism

Basic Principle: Stages of formation are interspersed with special services to mark movement from one stage to the next.

Stage	Service
1. Inquiry	1. Welcoming Hearers
2. Formation	2. Calling Persons to Baptism
3. Intensive Preparation	3. Holy Baptism
4. Integration into the Community	4. Affirmation of Ministry

After a period of mutual discernment among the inquirer, the sponsor, and other church representatives, if the inquirer expresses a desire to proceed further into Christian discipleship, then she or he participates in a worship service called "A Service for Welcoming Hearers." In this service, the inquirer is asked directly, "What do you seek?" and is given an opportunity to reply, "I seek life in Jesus Christ" or "I seek to know Jesus Christ," or a similar response. The inquirer also makes a public acceptance of the gospel, pledging a readiness to live a Christian life, a willingness to attend worship regularly, and a desire to hear the Word of God and to open her or his heart to welcome Jesus as Lord and Savior. This first public statement of emerging Christian commitment by the inquirer in the presence of the congregation changes her or his status in the initiation process to that of a "hearer." The designation comes from the inquirer's consecration to actively hear the Word of God as she or he seeks the way of Christ more fully.

After the service for welcoming, the hearer enters the stage of formation, which is a time of intentional, regular, and disciplined exploration of the Christian faith. The level of seriousness goes up a notch as the church becomes very focused in reproducing its faith and life in the hearer. This stage is characterized by regular meetings with catechists in "formational group sessions" or other educational settings, as well as with individual sponsors. (A sponsor's role during this time will be covered in much more detail in Chapters Three and Four; a sponsor's task during the different worship services will be considered in Chapter Two.) Notice that the level of resolution is also reflected in central questions posed to hearers: "Do you seek baptism?" and "Do you desire life with the church?" Having declared, in the service of welcoming hearers, her or his willingness to accept the gospel, the hearer now becomes focused on a fuller Christian commitment of faith.

When a hearer is ready for this fuller statement of faith in Christ, she or he can participate in the second special service, "A Service for Calling Persons to Baptism." In this service each hearer formally declares a desire to seek baptism. Since every sponsor is called upon to affirm her or his hearer's readiness to receive baptism and to make the appropriate confession of faith in this service, sponsors must have observed in time the hearer's growth in faith to make this witness truthfully. This service is often connected to particular times in the church year, preferably the first Sunday of Lent or perhaps the first Sunday of Advent. After this service a hearer is considered a candidate for baptism.

At this point the stage of intensive preparation for baptism begins. This period lasts only a few short weeks, but its work can last for eternity. Sponsors, catechists, and others assist candidates in addressing the crucial issues of Christian faith raised by the baptismal service itself: renouncing evil and sin, and confessing Jesus Christ as Lord and Savior. This time may involve the "handing on" of certain items in the church's treasury, such as the Apostles' Creed and the Lord's Prayer. It may include special rites where these riches are symbolically shared with candidates, and it may include special instruction in their meaning by catechists. Special prayer and fasting by and for the candidates by other church members may also be part of this stage of intensive preparation.

Finally, this period culminates in the service of baptism itself, preferably at the Easter Vigil (or on Easter Day) or on the Sunday of the Baptism of the Lord. Joy abounds on these occasions! But this culmination is not a conclusion. In a way the journey has just begun for both the newly baptized and her or his sponsor. Because a sponsor makes a pledge during the baptismal service, there is a continuing commitment by a sponsor to support the new member in her or his Christian life.

The baptismal service is followed by a stage of joyful investigation in how the newly baptized will follow Christ, specifically by fulfilling her or his ministry in the church. Of course, a sponsor, who should be very familiar with the baptismal charge by now, is crucial in helping to make this discernment. Special attention may be given to the meaning of the sacraments of baptism and Holy Communion as the basis for Christian living, the ground for Christian identity, and the nourishment for Christian ministry. This period will last several weeks; for example, in the case of baptisms performed at Easter, this period will last for seven weeks, the time between Easter and Pentecost.

Note that part of the task of the sponsor during this final stage is to work herself or himself out of a job. Since the goal is to fully integrate the newly baptized into the fellowship and ministry of the congregation, a perceptive sponsor will look for ways to slip out of the role of being the main link between the newly baptized and the congregation. The time has come for the new member to depend more directly upon her or his own relationship with the congregation.

A final service concludes the formally structured initiation process, one that affirms the ministry of the newly baptized. Since Christ's ministry has been shared with the whole church and since the church's ministry is shared among all its members, it is appropriate to recognize the newest member's part in Christian ministry. In this way the service anticipates the next and final stage—fruitful, faithful Christian living unto eternity. To resurrect this book's initial image, once one is in the house, it is only the beginning of a lifetime of enjoying God's blessings within the family of God.

A similar rhythm exists for another common scenario: when those already baptized desire a much fuller involvement in the church and a closer walk with Christ. These people may have diverse church backgrounds, including those baptized as children but never really integrated and involved in an active Christian life. It may also include those baptized at one time under their own confession of faith but who experienced a deep disconnection from the church. Their return would be a true homecoming.

Regardless of the returnee's background, the rhythm of stages and services will parallel those for people never previously baptized. The difference will be that with those previously baptized, the church recognizes them as members through baptism but also acknowledges the necessity for their full conversion and faith in Christ.

Figure 2 shows how the rhythm of stages and services for the returning member parallels that for unbaptized initiates. (The particular services will be reviewed in depth in Chapter Two.)

Figure 2

**The Rhythm of Stages and Services for Persons
Returning to the Baptismal Covenant**

Basic Principle: Stages of formation are interspersed with special services to
mark movement from one stage to the next.

Stage	*Service*
1. Inquiry	1. Welcoming a Returning Member
2. Formation in Faith and Ministry	2. Calling the Baptized to Continuing Conversion
3. Immediate Preparations for Affirmation of the Baptismal Covenant	3. Affirmation of the Baptismal Covenant
4. Call to Mission and Reflection on the Sacraments	4. Affirmation of Ministry

---

A similar rhythm—although with some shifts—is appropriate in another common scenario: instances in which the person to be baptized is an infant or child not yet able to confess faith on her or his own. The most important of these shifts is the awareness that the formation needs to be not only for the child but also for the parents who are to provide the committed Christian atmosphere for the ongoing spiritual formation of the child.

Thus, when children are baptized, the initiation process has two goals. First, the child is to be welcomed as a hearer of the Word, then baptized, subsequently formed in faith and discipleship—probably over the course of many years—until she or he is able to recognize and accept personally the grace God offers in baptism. Second, the initiation process should help form the parents as the primary sponsors for the children.

In practice, these two goals mean that the pre-baptismal formation is mainly directed toward the parents, rather than the child, while the post-baptismal formation is directed toward the child. Additionally, in most instances the post-baptismal formation takes place over the course of many years rather than the few weeks needed in the case of a newly-baptized adult. The basic rhythm for the baptism of children can be sketched in the following manner:

Figure 3

The Rhythm of Stages and Services for the Initiation of Children

Basic Principle: Stages of formation are interspersed with special services to mark movement from one stage to the next.

Stage	*Service*
1. Parental Inquiry Concerning Baptism of Children	1. Welcome of Children as Hearers, Through the Parent(s)
2. Preparation of the Parent(s) for Baptism of the Child	2. Calling Children to Baptism, Through the Parent(s)
3. Preparation for Baptism of the Child and for the Responsibilities Accepted at Baptism	3. Holy Baptism
4. Formation of the Child in Faith and Discipleship	4. Confirmation and Affirmation of Ministry

When children are baptized, the parents are the primary providers of ongoing Christian guidance, representing both God's care and the church's. Thus, the main responsibility of *church* sponsors, or godparents (if that term is used), is to assist *parents* in the formation process of the children. Additionally, as discussed earlier in the chapter, it is possible to use church sponsors more directly as the baptized children begin to prepare for confirmation and affirmation of ministry. Specifics of all of these responsibilities will be discussed in the chapters that follow.

QUESTIONS FOR REFLECTION

❧ Is it true that at times everyone's responsibility generally ends up being no one's responsibility? If so, how important is the role of the sponsor? In what way is a sponsor's role in initiation the task of the whole church?

❧ What insights do you receive from thinking of baptism not only as the one-time application of water but also as *the whole process* of "full immersion in Christ, the reign of God, and the church," with the purpose of truly forming someone as a Christian? What are the consequences of viewing baptism in this way?

❧ What do you think of the image of the "intricate art of gospel-living" as being learned by "apprenticeship" to "master" Christians? Is it true that one "learns to fast, pray, repent, celebrate, and serve the good of one's neighbor less by being lectured on these matters than by close association with people who do these things with regular ease and flair"? Has this way of learning by association been true in your own life? What are the implications for the role of a sponsor?

❧ What is the role of time in baptism? Who should determine the timing for baptism? What should be the main considerations in scheduling a baptism? More broadly, has there been a danger on the part of some people to see baptism mainly as a family event rather than primarily as a church event?

Chapter Two

WORSHIP RESPONSIBILITIES
OF A SPONSOR

SPONSORS, INTEGRITY, AND WORSHIP

Worship services be can described in flattering (moving and inspiring) or not-so-flattering terms (cold and irrelevant). Another word best describes the worship services of baptism and initiation: integrity.

We can be certain that God's promises are always fulfilled. God is true to the Word of God. From God's standpoint, worship is always filled with integrity. This chapter focuses on the human responses called for in the services of initiation. Will we be true to our promises?

How significant these promises are! Review the baptismal service. The pledges of commitment made by the new initiate are truly awesome: renouncing evil, rejecting wickedness, and adhering to Christ as Savior and Lord. The pre-baptismal formation is designed to prepare the initiate for making these pledges with the highest level of integrity. Worship services provide the horizon for the preceding activities.

But it is not only the one being baptized who makes these pledges; the sponsor makes them as well. The commitments made by a sponsor are numerous, weighty, and significant. In every worship service of initiation, sponsors play a prominent role. The services are full of statements and actions where sponsors play key roles. Through these, a sponsor represents the church and the gospel to the initiate, and represents the initiate to the church. Both presentations are called for at various times during the services.

The sponsor's role in the services sets the framework for his or her activity throughout the initiation process. What takes place within worship should determine what occurs outside of worship. Will there be a consistency between a sponsor's activities, both in and out of worship? Will pledges of support be fulfilled? Will a sponsor's gestures of welcome and care to the initiate continue on a day-to-day basis? Will a sponsor's affirmation that his or her candidate is ready for baptism be true?

These are only some of the concerns. Sponsors should be well aware of their responsibilities in the worship services so that they can fulfill them with integrity. This chapter examines the basic worship activities that sponsors are called upon to do. The chapter concludes with a step-by-step commentary on specific sponsor activities within each service.

A SPONSOR'S BASIC WORSHIP ROLE: PRESENTATION

A sponsor plays a notable role in the initiation worship services, one that is most enjoyable. Sponsors generally act as gift-givers. The services repeatedly rely upon sponsors to present the most precious of gifts. What could be more enjoyable?

As noted in the first chapter, a sponsor's presentations flow in two directions. First, at times a sponsor exemplifies the church and the Lord in presenting gifts to the initiate. He or she represents the church by offering pledges, gestures used in worship, and sometimes objects as the believing community acts on behalf of its Savior, Christ. These presentations are made as if they come from the heart of the church and from the hand of God.

But a sponsor also makes presentations to the church on behalf of his or her initiate and, in so doing, presents the initiate to the congregation. At times, this means that the sponsor formally introduces the initiate to the congregation. This, too, is offered as ultimately a gift of God. What could be a better gift to the church than God's renewal through new life?

Figure 4 summarizes the kinds of presentations sponsors make in worship. Let us examine them in more detail.

Figure 4

Sponsor's Presentations in Worship Services

From church to initiate:	From initiate to church:
Accompaniment	*Accompaniment*
—Escorts initiate	—Stays and moves with initiate
Gestures	*Statements*
—Laying on of hands during prayer	—Names and introduces initiate
—Tracing sign of the cross	—Attests to readiness to be received
—Giving Bible	
(perhaps candle and clothing)	
Statements	
—Commitments of support and care	

As mentioned before, a sponsor's presentations to the initiate on the church's behalf are threefold. The first is the most basic of sponsorial responsibilities: A sponsor accompanies his or her initiate during the special worship services. Based on instructions in the services, initiates are not to be left unattended. When initiates stand before the congregation, sponsors are to escort them.

Such a simple act is not without great significance, and its gift is presence and companionship. By being with the initiate, a sponsor serves as a tangible link between the church and the initiate and makes evident the church's love and God's love.

This aspect of tangibility is at the heart of the second category of sponsorial presentation to initiates. During some public services, a sponsor is called upon to place a hand on the shoulder of the initiate during the welcoming prayer. Through this gesture the concern of the church—and the concern of a loving God—is made visible by the simple, palpable act of the sponsor. (The laying on of hands is an ancient and biblical gesture of blessing and consecration.) Similarly, a sponsor may be called upon at times to trace the sign of the cross on the initiate's forehead to indicate the way of Christ accepted by him or her.

Other gestures are sometimes recommended. In the service for welcoming hearers, for example, sponsors may give Bibles to the hearers. If a congregation decides to make other presentations—for example, baptismal candles or new clothing as allowed in the baptismal service—sponsors should be the ones bestowing these.[11]

Finally, sponsors make a verbal commitment to support and help initiates on behalf of the church. Repeatedly, sponsors are asked if they will assist initiates in their spiritual formation. These commitments are essential because they make specific and clear the nurturing concern of the church for each newcomer. In this way a sponsor serves as a representative of the church. The specific commitment of the sponsor expresses, but does *not* substitute for, the church's nurturing commitment.

Similarly, a sponsor makes presentations to the church on the *initiate's* behalf through accompaniment and formal introduction. Having a sponsorial escort during the worship services represents the church's welcome to the initiate and establishes for the membership an unspoken link between the initiate and a fellow member.

A sponsor formally introduces an initiate to the membership at crucial points (especially at worship services) during the initiation process. The initial presentation typically occurs at the first service, when the sponsor stands before the congregation and says, "I present *(name of the initiate or family)*." (Note that a sponsor makes a similar presentation during the baptismal service.) The church is dependent upon a sponsor to introduce the initiate; an initiate, likewise, is dependent upon a sponsor for introduction to the household of faith. By this simple act of presentation, a sponsor is assumed to know everyone involved—the initiate and the church.

At a later service, a sponsor must vouch for the candidate's readiness to receive baptism, and that requires familiarity. Much that follows in the initiation process, specifically the further preparation for membership, relies upon the sponsor's honest assessment. (Factors to be considered in the sponsor's discernment at this point will be explored in Chapter Four.)

With this overview of a sponsor's role in worship completed, let us now focus on the specific services for initiates. A brief commentary on each service is provided. Although reading the entire section would be informative to any sponsor, you should study more closely the part that deals with the type of initiate you are helping: adults preparing for baptism, parents preparing for the baptism of children, or others returning to the baptismal covenant. A final section deals with the situation of someone transferring into a local congregation.

A SPONSOR'S ROLE IN THE
SERVICES FOR ADULTS SEEKING BAPTISM

As noted in Chapter One, at least four services are involved in the baptismal preparation for those who can speak for themselves. (See *Come to the Waters*, pp. 109-121 for the text of the services. Quotations are taken from these services. The baptismal service itself can be found in either *The United Methodist Hymnal* [pp. 33-39] or *The United Methodist Book of Worship* [pp. 86-94].)

1. A SERVICE FOR WELCOMING HEARERS

The first service is "A Service for Welcoming Hearers," where a sponsor is called upon to make the presentations discussed previously.

Before the service begins, the sponsors gather with the inquirers, preferably outside the church or in an entry area. A sponsor should stand with his or her initiate. The service starts when the presiding and assisting ministers, including catechists, join and greet the inquirers. After these informal greetings, the group moves to the sanctuary where the congregation is assembled. When called upon by the presiding minister, a sponsor begins the formal part of the service by saying, "I present *(name)*, who desires to learn the way of Christ."

A period of questioning follows. First the presiding minister and catechist ask the inquirer about his or her basic desire and willingness to hear the gospel. When the inquirer has answered with his or her commitment, the sponsor and the members are then called upon to make their own commitment to the inquirer. Specifically, they promise to care for the inquirer "with...prayer and companionship" and to help the inquirer "by word and example to know God and to discover the way of following Jesus Christ." These questions are addressed to both the congregation and sponsor: to the congregation because it has the God-given responsibility to provide a nurturing atmosphere; and to the sponsor because he or she serves as the church's representative to the initiate.

Following this commitment, the pastor, or other leader, prays a prayer that welcomes the inquirer as a hearer and that helps everyone remember how such an act of welcome expresses God's love. During the prayer, the sponsor lays his or her hand on the shoulder of the inquirer, a tangible expression of this love.

The hearer is further set apart by the next act of worship. As the presiding minister speaks about being marked by the sign of the cross as an indication of following Christ, the sponsor is called upon to trace a cross on the hearer's forehead. (A light touch on the forehead with the thumb is perhaps best.) The service also suggests the option of marking the sign of the cross on the hearer's ears, eyes, lips, heart, shoulders, hands, and feet to demonstrate a full dedication of the whole person to the way of Jesus Christ.

One final tangible presentation culminates the service. As someone speaks about the importance of the Word of God, a sponsor may present a Bible to his or her hearer. (Remember that initiates who have completed this service are called hearers.)

This service concludes with the hearers and sponsors taking their seats and participating in the remainder of that day's worship. It is good for the sponsors to stay with the hearers. Although a simple thing, remaining together while engaged in worship reinforces the bond between the hearer and sponsor.

2. A SERVICE FOR CALLING PERSONS TO BAPTISM

The next service occurs at the beginning of the period set apart for intensive preparation and is called "A Service for Calling Persons to Baptism." It takes place after a period of continuing Christian formation of the hearer, guided by the catechist and sponsor. This service includes a witness by the sponsor about the hearer's readiness to be baptized. Therefore, it must be preceded by appropriate discussion and discernment among the sponsor, the hearer, the catechist, and the pastor. (A discussion of the discernment process is found in Chapter Four.)

The service is normally celebrated after the sermon during morning worship. The sponsor's first act is that of accompaniment: sponsors and catechists come forward with the hearers when summoned. Sponsors should stand with the person they assist.

This service begins with the catechist's presentation of all the hearers. The next action is the heart of the matter and one of the most important responsibilities of a sponsor. After the pastor charges the sponsors to tell of the hearers' readiness "to obey Christ's call to life in the baptismal covenant," the sponsors witness to the hearers' faithful participation in worship, to their having heard God's Word, to their having followed Jesus Christ in daily life, to their knowing the story and way of Jesus Christ, and, finally, to their being engaged in ministry with "the poor and the neglected." Some congregations will also give sponsors an opportunity at this point to speak directly concerning the hearers' growth in grace. In such a case a sponsor should choose his or her words carefully so as to neither praise nor embarrass the hearer but to give witness to the goodness of God at work within the hearer.

After a charge to the congregation and verbal acceptance by the candidates (the term for hearers from this point on) to move toward baptism, the service concludes with several actions by the sponsors. Sponsors are again commissioned to support the candidates during the coming period of intensive preparation. Acceptance on the part of the sponsors is implicit in the service. Finally, as prayers are said for the candidates, sponsors place hands on the candidates' shoulders as the presiding minister prays. After the prayer, sponsors accompany their candidates through the remainder of worship.

Three rites may occur during the period of intensive preparation. The first two involve a "handing on" of some of the church's "treasures": the Apostles' Creed and the Lord's Prayer. These services are beautiful and moving. They can make quite an impression as the church demonstrates its acceptance of the candidates by sharing with them the two items at the heart of the church's life. Sponsors stand with the candidates during these rites. If written copies of the Apostles' Creed and the Lord's Prayer are given, it would be appropriate (if the congregation so chooses) for the sponsor to present them.

The third rite, which may be performed during the time of intensive preparation, is called "Examination of Conscience." Basically, this rite centers on prayer. The congregation asks God to lovingly fulfill the candidates' inner spiritual transformation. Sponsors accompany their candidates, remaining with them and possibly even kneeling with them during the prayer. Sponsors also extend the gesture of blessing and consecration by placing their hands on the shoulders of the candidates during prayer.

3. HOLY BAPTISM

The period of intensive preparation culminates in the administration of baptism. A sponsor's role during this service is similar to those before. Once again, a sponsor accompanies the candidate through the service. After the pastor's greeting begins the service, the sponsor presents the candidate to the congregation, saying, "I present *(name)* for baptism." A sponsor renews the vow to "support and encourage" his or her candidate, again showing Christian love. If other offerings are to be made (a gift of new clothing or a candle after baptism), the sponsor should make these presentations to the candidate. Even when instructions for the service do not specifically mention them, sponsors may play a prominent role in other aspects of the service. For example, a sponsor may place a hand on the shoulder of his or her candidate during prayer or be among the first to exchange an act of peace and welcome after the candidate's baptism.

4. A SERVICE FOR AFFIRMATION OF MINISTRY IN DAILY LIFE

This is the final service for the newly baptized. Following a period of reflection to find a sense of calling in the weeks after baptism, the newly baptized person participates in this service. It is designed to recognize and affirm his or her place in the congregation's life and ministry. "An Order for Commitment to Christian Service," in *The United Methodist Book of Worship* (591-592) is one possibility for this service.

In this service of affirmation a sponsor continues to assume his or her presenting role. Each new member should be accompanied by a sponsor. If deemed appropriate, the sponsor may be called upon to provide testimony about the God-given gifts and ministries the newly baptized person brings to the congregation's life for the benefit of its service to the world. If a prayer of consecration is made on behalf of the newly baptized, the sponsor may be expected to lay hands on the person.

A SPONSOR'S ROLE IN THE SERVICES
FOR PARENTS SEEKING BAPTISM OF CHILDREN

Sponsors who accompany parents preparing for the baptism of children should remember that this scenario uses the same pattern as the one for the stages of preparation and worship services for adults seeking baptism (see Chapter One). Many of the sponsorial worship responsibilities are the same as well. Because the parents and their child are in the process of being formed in the Christian faith, a sponsor is called upon to be the "middle man" between the congregation, the parents, and the child. In other words, presentations on behalf of the congregation will be offered only to the parents at times and only to the child at other times. The following commentary will highlight the occasions when this shift happens. (For the text of these services, see *Come to the Waters*, pp. 130-137. Unless otherwise noted, all quotations are taken from this text.)

1. A SERVICE FOR WELCOMING A CHILD AS A HEARER

This is the first service in the process of initiating children into the community of the baptized. (Remember that even if the process of initiation is abbreviated by eliminating the services before baptism [something not recommended here], the notion of presentation still accurately describes a sponsor's responsibility in the baptismal service.) Typically a sponsor's first act in this service is accompaniment. He or she stays with the parents and the child throughout the service. After an initial greeting by the pastor, a sponsor makes the formal presentation to the church by saying, "I present the *(family name)* family who desires this child, *(child's name)*, to know and follow Christ."

The service continues with the parents expressing a desire to seek the life or knowledge of Christ for their child and pledging to provide a Christian context for the child's upbringing. Notice that one of the parents' pledges is to sponsor the child. In this way, the service recognizes that parents are naturally the primary sponsors of their child's Christian formation. But the parents are not alone in this responsibility. Following the parents' pledges, the sponsor and the congregation are asked to present themselves to the parents as caring helpmates in shaping the child as a Christian.

The service concludes with several familiar gestures of love by the sponsor, including the laying on of hands during prayer. Next a sponsor traces the sign of the cross on the forehead of the hearer (the child) as the presiding minister speaks about the cross as the sign of Christ. If the optional tracing of a cross on other parts of the hearer's body is selected, a sponsor should do this also. The service concludes with the presentation of a Bible to the hearer by his or her sponsor. After this presentation a sponsor should remain with the family as they take their seats.

2. A SERVICE FOR CALLING CHILDREN TO BAPTISM, THROUGH THEIR PARENTS

This second worship service normally occurs after an extended period of Christian formation for the parents. Instructions for the service presume that a sponsor will stand with the parents and hearer, the child.

In this service, sponsors deliver the crucial spoken presentation to the church on behalf of the parents and the hearer. To uphold the integrity of the impending baptism, the congregation asks each sponsor to attest to the parents' faithful participation in worship, their hearing of the Word of God and its application in daily life, and their having learned the story and way of Christ so that they are "engaged in ministry with the poor and the neglected." In addition to answering these questions, sponsors may be asked to witness to the "growth and courage of the hearers or their parents in learning the Christian life." As the service suggests, the sponsor's witness should represent God's love and should not be embarrassing or excessive in praise.

The witness by the sponsor is the foundation for several other acts of commitment made in the service. After a statement from the congregation that it will continue to support the parents and the hearers, the parents of hearers not able to answer for themselves are asked to specifically state their desire to seek baptism for the children. Sponsors, then, receive a charge to continue to support the parents and the candidate—the status has now changed from hearer to candidate—in keeping the disciplines that open us to the grace of God. Although no spoken response is called for by the instructions of the service, the implication is that the sponsors commit themselves to this charge.

The service concludes with a prayer offered for the candidates for baptism. As in other services, the sponsor and the parents place their hands on the shoulder of the candidate. When the parents and the candidate return to their seats or leave to meet in their formational groups, the sponsor should accompany them.

3. HOLY BAPTISM

In the service of baptism a sponsor is called upon to perform many familiar sponsorial roles. (The service to be used if there are no baptisms of adults is found in *The United Methodist Book of Worship*, pp. 95-99, or in *The United Methodist Hymnal*, pp. 39-43.) The service presumes that the sponsor will accompany the parents and the candidates through the baptismal service. At the beginning of the service, the sponsor presents the candidate by name to the congregation for baptism. As in previous services, the sponsor commits to support and encourage the newly baptized in his or her Christian life. Sponsors can join the parents in pledging to nurture the child in the congregation until the child professes faith on his or her own. If the congregation chooses, sponsors may also be called upon to present certain objects, such as new baptismal clothing, to the newly baptized. If a congregation elects to extend acts of welcome and peace to the newly baptized, a sponsor may offer a kiss or another gesture of love.

The sponsor's representative role is particularly important in baptisms for children because they are unable to speak for themselves. This role is emphasized at key points in the service. For example, in committing to nurture the child "in Christ's holy church" (*The United Methodist Hymnal*, p. 34), the sponsor acts as a representative of the congregation's care, example, and teaching. Likewise, if the church so chooses, a sponsor may receive on behalf of the child the lighted baptismal candle after the sacrament. (The instructions also allow the parents to receive the candle; in this case it is best if the sponsor presents the candle.)

4. A SERVICE OF CONFIRMATION AND AFFIRMATION OF MINISTRY IN DAILY LIFE

This is the final service in the process of the initiation of children in the life and ministry of the congregation. Many years have passed since baptism. Time is necessary for the child to be formed in the Christian faith and to become mature enough to confess faith in Christ on his or her own. The appropriate service is "The Baptismal Covenant I" in either *The United Methodist Hymnal* (pp. 33-39) or *The United Methodist Book of Worship* (pp. 86-94). Although this service is not a rebaptism and the water should not be administered in a way that implies rebaptism, it is good for the young people to go through the basic baptismal service, making the pledges of the covenant for themselves.

A sponsor's role in this service is very similar to the one performed during the baptismal service. Sponsorial presentations on behalf of the congregation include accompaniment, statements of continuing support, and extended gestures of welcome and blessing. A congregation may also choose to present tangible gifts to the confirmands. The service offers some latitude. Presentations on behalf of the young people to the congregation include a formal presentation by name at the beginning of the service.

A SPONSOR'S ROLE IN SERVICES FOR
PERSONS RETURNING TO THE BAPTISMAL COVENANT

As noted in Chapter One, not everyone is baptized as a child (or as an adult) and lives a life that is deeply dedicated to Christ and actively involved in the church. For many, these two points (baptism and active following of Christ) are separated by a period of time. *Come to the Waters* notes that these "separated members" typically fall in one of three categories:

- those baptized as children but never fully integrated into the life of the church
- those baptized on their own profession of faith but who have fallen away from active Christian discipleship
- those who at one time were active, baptized Christian disciples but who, subsequently, had adhered to a non-Christian religion or way or life, or were otherwise estranged from the church[12]

For all of these people, the initiation process is actually one of *integration*. This word comes from a Latin root with a wide range of similar, positive meanings: wholeness, soundness, renewal, refreshment, among others. The integration of members who were once baptized but subsequently slipped away recreates a sense of wholeness. For the congregation, it is renewing to graft these members back into active discipleship; for the individuals involved, it is renewing to find one's place in the household of faith.

As discussed in Chapter One, the rhythm of stages and services is similar to that used for adults not previously baptized. The tone is a little different, however. Instead of anticipating the grace that God shares in baptism, as in the case of an unbaptized adult, the services focus on fulfilling the grace already given in baptism by having these persons progressively accept the baptismal covenant. Sponsors will notice that sometimes the services for their charges are held at times different from services for unbaptized initiates. This is done to avoid confusion between the unbaptized and the baptized. Sponsors of the previously baptized will also notice, however, that the basic presentations in the respective services remain the same.

1. A SERVICE FOR WELCOMING A RETURNING MEMBER

The sponsor's role for this first service parallels that of the other services of welcome discussed previously. The fundamental presentation is that the sponsor is with the inquirer through the entire service. The service begins when the sponsor formally presents the baptized inquirer by name to the congregation.

Several questions to the returning member follow. These questions concern what the inquirer is seeking and whether he or she will commit to being involved in the church's fellowship, worship, service, and calling for justice and peace. To ensure that the inquirer does not perceive his or her commitment as a solitary matter, the sponsor is immediately called upon to present the congregation's commitment to the inquirer. Sponsors are questioned about their willingness to support and help the inquirers' growth in grace, followed by a similar commitment on the part of the entire congregation. Afterward, the pastor prays for God's blessing on the returning members. To represent the congregation's love and God's love, sponsors place a hand on the shoulder of their charges during this prayer.

Instructions for the service provide for the presentation of a Bible to each returning member. As in the case of the other welcoming services, the Bible is perhaps best presented by the sponsor, although the instructions do not specifically call for this.

2. A SERVICE CALLING THE BAPTIZED TO CONTINUING CONVERSION

In the second service for those seeking to reaffirm the baptismal covenant, returning members are presented before the congregation as those seeking restoration to the way of Christ. When done in a larger worship setting, preferably the worship on Ash Wednesday, this context sets a wonderful stage for the returning members' experience. What the congregation generally commits to at the beginning of Lent—a renewed dedication to the spiritual disciplines that lead to the grace of God—is exemplified specifically in the quest of returning members. Thus, sponsors are called upon to make another formal presentation of the returning members by saying, "I present *(name)* who desires to journey with us by self-examination and repentance and to be restored to the way of Christ. *He/she* is ready to join us as we give ourselves to Christ during these forty days."[13] Sponsors may also give public witness to the increasing faithfulness and discipline on the part of the returning members.

In the period of intensive preparation following the second service, returning members prepare for and anticipate affirming the baptismal covenant at the Easter Vigil. A special service called "A Celebration of Reconciliation" (*Come to the Waters,* pp. 148-150) provides a wonderful opportunity for returning members and the congregation to celebrate publicly their reconciliation and "the restoration of their life together as the people of God" (*Come to the Waters,* p. 148). The preferred occasion for the service is Holy Thursday. Other than the responsibility of accompanying the returning member, a sponsor has no specific duties in the service. However, if a congregation chooses to include special gestures of reconciliation, the sponsors would be a natural choice to make these gestures.

3. A SERVICE OF AFFIRMATION OF THE BAPTISMAL COVENANT

The next pivotal worship experience for returning members is to participate in the service of the baptismal covenant. This service can be found in *The United Methodist Hymnal* (pp. 33-39) and in *The United Methodist Book of Worship* (pp. 86-94). Of course, returning members will not be rebaptized, but they can participate in many of the spoken parts of the service. A sponsor's role during this service is similar to that of sponsors who accompany candidates for baptism. All sponsors should accompany their initiates. The service, after an initial greeting, opens with each sponsor presenting his or her charge by name. In this case, a sponsor would say, "I present *(name of the returning member)* to reaffirm *their* faith." During the service, sponsors are given an opportunity to present the congregation's care for returning members by pledging support and encouragement to them as they seek to follow Christ. Other specific acts are left to the discretion and creativity of the congregation. It would be more than appropriate, for instance, if sponsors placed a hand on the members during one of the prayers. A sponsor could also welcome the returning member with a sign of peace. Likewise, since the service allows for some flexibility in the use of water in reaffirming the baptismal covenant—as long as it cannot be interpreted as a rebaptism—sponsors may participate in this action too. (See the instructions in *The United Methodist Hymnal* [p. 37] or *The United Methodist Book of Worship* [pp. 92-93].)

4. A SERVICE FOR AFFIRMATION OF MINISTRY IN DAILY LIFE

The final special service for returning members is "An Order for Commitment to Christian Service," found in *The United Methodist Book of Worship* (591-592). A sponsor in this service performs many of the same duties of presentation, with accompaniment being the primary one. The church may also call upon each sponsor to give witness about how God has equipped the returning member for participating in the church's ministry. Any prayers and blessings may also be done with sponsors placing hands on the shoulders of their charges.

SPONSORS FOR TRANSFERRING MEMBERS

There is one other case in which sponsors may be used for new members: when people transfer membership from another church. Although this situation is not the real focus of this book or its companion volumes, it is appropriate to consider the responsibilities of this kind of sponsor. Beyond worship, much of the sponsor responsibilities discussed in Chapter Three and Chapter Four will be applicable.

Is it necessary to have sponsors when new members are merely transferring from another church? No, but it is helpful. When used to receive transferring members, "The Baptismal Covenant I" service (*The United Methodist Hymnal,* pp. 33-39) presumes a sponsor performing a worship role. The service calls for a sponsor to present the transferring member, as well as to pledge support and encouragement to the member. In my pastoral experience, having sponsors has been a helpful and moving practice. Within worship, sponsors represent a visible link between the new member and the church; outside of worship, it is helpful to have someone who provides a natural, specific point of incorporation for the new member.

QUESTIONS FOR REFLECTION

❧ Is it helpful to make a sponsor's activities in worship the basis for his or her activities outside worship? If *presentation* is the central notion of a sponsor's worship activities, how would you expect this to be lived out with an initiate outside of worship? Generally, what should be the connection between what we do in worship and how we live daily?

❧ What are the different ways a sponsor makes the congregation's concern for an initiate visible to him or her? Do you see this as a particularly important task? Would you agree that people know love not only by hearing someone speak about it but also by seeing it in others? If so, and if the church ultimately reflects God's love, how important is the task of a sponsor?

❧ This chapter has presented the basic worship responsibility of the sponsor as *presentation*. Are there other words or phrases that summarize the sponsor's responsibility in a more vivid way for you?

Chapter Three

THE SPONSOR'S ROLE OF PRESENTING THE CHURCH AS GRACED COMMUNITY

GRACE WITH A FACE: SPONSORS AND THE CHURCH

In the early days of Methodism, a young man from upstate New York, William Keith, questioned how he could experience the grace of God. Keith was perplexed. He understood how Jesus Christ could offer God's love when he lived among the people of Galilee, reaching out, blessing the people, and assuring them that their sins were forgiven. But how can the same grace be offered since Jesus' Ascension? Keith wrote a spiritual autobiography outlining his conclusion.[14]

Keith resolved that God continues to touch lives through a person's association with and activity in the church. The church assigns a face and hands and feet to the love of God. What Keith discovered has been encountered by millions of people over two thousand years of history: An individual's experience of God's grace is often closely related to her or his sense of the church. The church makes specific and concrete God's grace in the world. The church points beyond itself to God and to God's reign.

But it goes a step beyond that. As Keith noted, his experience of the church as graced community was not merely an encounter with a church in general but also with individual members. Keith's association with certain people was critical. As the church makes specific and tangible the love of God, its members make specific and tangible the gracious nature of the church. For example, an exhorter (an early Methodist worship tradition) well known to Keith made quite an impression on his faith. Because Keith had known the man for a long time, he could see the difference the gospel had made in the exhorter's life. That made Keith more open to what the exhorter was saying.

A great mystery made possible by the sheer graciousness of God is evident: When faithful Christians manifest God's grace in their lives, others can experience God's grace. Although not limited to Methodists, this truth is apparent in the stories of the early Methodist tradition. Often the power of this mystery is portrayed by a tension—implicit in Keith's experience with his exhorter friend. To those who yearn to encounter God's grace, Christians who have already experienced grace are both familiar and unfamiliar. In one sense, these Christians are peers, recognizable and well-known. Yet, as the Methodist stories repeatedly depict, God's grace make them more than peers, showing that there is a quality of life available that can be made abundant by the grace of God.

Ideally, and by the grace of God, this tension is what a sponsor can provide to an initiate. On one hand, sponsors are peers. They breathe the same air, enjoy the same sun, live in the same place, eat the same foods, face the same temptations, and struggle with the same concerns. It is hoped that the sponsor is someone to whom the initiate can truly relate. But, on the other hand, a sponsor should bring more to the relationship: namely, a walk with Christ and a knowledge of what it means to enjoy the love of God. These should become accessible to the initiate through the presence of a kind and loving sponsor who wishes to share them.

This theme will be discussed in terms of the now-familiar idea of *presentation*. Remember that presentation of the church *to* the candidate is fundamental to the "job description" of a sponsor. As we saw in Chapter One:

> The sponsor makes specific and concrete the attitude of the church, and, through the church, the ultimately gracious welcome of God. In other words, the sponsor represents (re-*presents*) to each newcomer the Christian attitudes that the church holds for its new members: welcome, concern, support, love, and accountability. An initiate should see these things in her or his sponsor.

In Chapter Two we reviewed a sponsor's specific actions that fulfilled this role during worship. It is now proper to discuss a sponsor's role of presenting the church to the initiate outside of worship. In this chapter, we will explore many images representing this idea and give practical suggestions to help sponsors fulfill this role.

Above all, sponsors should remember this: What the church is to the newcomers *generally*, based on the love of God, the sponsor should be *specifically*. This notion is the basic principle behind a sponsor's role of presenting the church to the initiate. Sponsors are not substitutes for the congregation. They are representatives of the church. The ministry of initiation belongs to the entire church.

THE SPONSOR AS BRIDGE

A bridge is one of the simplest, yet most useful structures we have in our environment. In like manner, a sponsor serves as one of the simplest, yet most useful ministries in the life of the congregation. A bridge covers a gap, or chasm, by providing a physical link between two points. A sponsor spans any gap that exists between the initiate and the church by providing a symbolic link between the two.

This role has been stressed vigorously in the past. As we will see in the last chapter, some churches have not allowed potential candidates to apply for preparation for baptism unless they first had sponsors. So emphasized was a sponsor's role as a bridge that she or he literally appeared to be the only link between the church and the person desiring baptism into Christ. Without a sponsor, a newcomer seemed to have no access to the church.

Although modern churches are not likely to emphasize the role of a sponsor as a bridge, the image is a useful one. The responsibility for making sure that an initiate has a connecting point to the church is one of the most basic sponsorial tasks.

Notice that as the charge becomes more fully integrated into the life of the congregation, this role may lessen for the sponsor. This is natural and desirable as the sense of distance between the charge and the congregation narrows.

IDEAS FOR BEING A BRIDGE

- Get to know your initiate well. Learn to understand what motivates her or him spiritually.
- Listen thoroughly. Be the congregation's "ear" to hear what deep questions your initiate brings to God. You do not have to know all the answers. With the initiate's permission and desire, use the written and personnel resources of the church to develop answers.
- Spend time with the initiate outside of scheduled church activities. Extend God's concern for her or him in daily life by visiting the initiate at home or in the workplace, if appropriate. Can recreational time be spent together?
- Provide a gentle reminder of required meetings and activities. Help your initiate shape her or his calendar.
- Consider sitting with the initiate during worship and other meetings.
- If the initiate is receptive, be open to talking about your own journey in the Christian faith, baptism, and entrance into the church. It is too easy to think of these things in the abstract. Be willing to put these matters in a personal, understandable form. Share the joys and anxieties you felt when facing these things.
- Just as the Gospels say, a decision to follow Christ sometimes results in strained family relations and other difficulties. Be attentive to the crosses that your initiate must bear in her or his decision to follow Christ. Be ready to bridge the gap, offering whatever support or assistance seems appropriate.
- What are your own ideas on how to be a bridge?

_____

_____

_____

_____

THE SPONSOR AS TOUR GUIDE

At first glance, the image of a sponsor as a tour guide may seem a little unusual. But do not discount the image without giving it some thought. For one thing, it is a venerable image for baptismal sponsors. Moreover, it is not meant to be taken literally. No one is advocating that sponsors pack their bags and lead a trip to the Holy Land (although that does sound like fun). But, typically, the average tour guide's job shares some similarities with sponsorial duties.

A guide is someone who helps a newcomer through an unfamiliar place. A trip is made much more meaningful for the tourists if the guide is experienced and knowledgeable about the area of interest.

The tour guide I remember above all is one who helped me really enjoy the sites of Pompeii. One summer I visited this town twice. The first time I was part of a very large group of tourists under the direction of one guide. The guide did his best, but the group's size and time constraints prevented a truly enjoyable, thorough visit. At times he could do little more than herd us. Dissatisfied, three of us decided we wanted another visit to Pompeii. A few weeks later we returned and hired our own tour guide. Able to do much more with a small group, this guide led us on a very complete tour of the city.

A good guide will accomplish three basic tasks. First, the guide will prevent anyone from getting lost. The guide uses prior knowledge and familiarity, along with a guiding presence, to make sure no one strays. Second, the guide provides direction and orientation. Even if it is never articulated, a good guide has a plan for moving forward and seeing things in an orderly manner. Third, a guide directs people's attention in the right direction to the right things at the right time, enhancing the meaning and appreciation of what is being observed. A good guide knows how to turn unfamiliarity and strangeness into newfound understanding and appreciation. From the guide's perspective, there is great joy when this experience is created; there is a deep sense of fulfillment in helping others enjoy what the guide experiences regularly.

A sponsor shares many of these same tasks. First, a sponsor's role is preventative. She or he must make sure that the initiate does not wander off. The sponsor ensures that the initiate stays active and committed to the formation process. Second, a sponsor should understand the goal of the formation process and should have a plan to assist the initiate in coming to a greater awareness of the wonders of God's love. A good sponsor has a sense of the progress to be made. Third, a sponsor works to turn the initiate's unfamiliarity with the things of God into newfound understanding and appreciation. A sponsor works to overcome the sense of strangeness that an initiate may feel as she or he travels deeper into the mysteries of God's love.

This image of a sponsor as a tour guide is closest to the title of this book, *Accompanying the Journey*. By being a guide a sponsor surely *accompanies* the initiate on her or his *journey* into full admission in the ways of Christ, the reign of God, and the body of Christ, which is the church. The title evokes some of the basic responsibilities of a good guide: a gentle, guiding presence who helps the initiate progress in grace and form a deeper appreciation of the wonder and love of God found in the church and in the world.

IDEAS FOR BEING A TOUR GUIDE

- Could parts of the services surprise the initiate? Be familiar with what will be done during the services. Make sure that the initiate knows what to expect.
- Take some time to become aware again of the mysteries of God and the wonders of the church. What has become too familiar to you? Reawaken your own sense of wonder, awe, and history. Resurrect your awareness of why it is exciting to be a Christian.
- Lead your initiate on a tour of your church or some other sacred space. Share your memories of the sacredness of the space. Begin to create deep associations for the initiate.
- Consider attending with your initiate some of the special services (weddings and/or funerals) that open the deepest issues about the nature of Christian hope

and expectations. Be open to discussing these issues.

- Take your initiate to churches of other Christian denominations. Use these experiences as points of reference to reflect more on the congregation to which you belong.
- Spend some time remembering the difficulties you may have experienced because you are an active follower of Christ. Be on the lookout for these difficulties in your initiate. Provide encouragement and assistance as appropriate.
- Keep tabs on the attendance patterns of your initiate, both in worship services and the formational group sessions. Do not be afraid to encourage accountability.
- What are your own ideas on how to be a tour guide?

_____

_____

_____

_____

THE SPONSOR AS HOST

At times, I have found it extremely difficult to join a group in which I had no contacts. It can be very intimidating to walk through a door, hoping to find a comfortable place within the group inside.

I experienced this once in college, and it was one of the hardest things I had ever done. I had become a United Methodist toward the end of high school and so, when I got to college, I wanted to join the Wesley Foundation (the United Methodist student center). But I did not know anyone in the Wesley Foundation. I can still remember vividly my anxiety as I stood across the street and looked at the front door. Finally, I walked across the street, stepped through the door, and found a group whose warmth and excitement eventually changed my relationship with God. A large part of that change was the work of certain members who greeted me with great hospitality and took me under their wings. Perhaps you are the sort of person who can take on this type of challenge with less anxiety. But I truly appreciated the welcome I received; without it, I am not sure I would have returned to the group.

Providing such hospitality is at the heart of a sponsor's role as host. As noted in the first chapter, it is an important part of a sponsor's task to offer the abundance of hospitality that God exhibits in the church. It is the sponsor's specific role to make sure that the initiate finds the church a hospitable place and group.

Many congregations recognize the importance of this and provide "greeters" to meet people on Sunday morning. Sponsors should be considered as greeters for the entire life of the church. The fundamental issues are those of hospitality: how to make the church congenial, open, accessible, and warm.

A good host normally provides several services, which a sponsor should imitate. First, she or he presents a warm reception for the guest. The host works hard to make guests feel welcome. Second, a host provides introductions, making sure others know the guest's name and vice versa. In some respects, our names are who we are. Thus, the first step of integration into a group is to be known by name. Third, a host ushers the guest to the abundance of provisions available. A truly good host can help a guest feel moved by the graciousness of the occasion.

A sponsor should fulfill the same role with her or his initiate. What a marvelous privilege—and responsibility—it is to be the one who ushers a seeker into the utter graciousness of God and all the blessings that God's grace has provided! Surely this role should be one of the most enjoyable for a sponsor.

IDEAS FOR BEING A HOST

- Always greet the initiate by name. Be intentional in greeting the initiate whenever you see her or him at church.
- Examine your own attitude. Do not let your own unfamiliarity with the initiate hold you back. Assume the actions of a good host, and allow the attitude to follow.
- What would your attitude be if you met your initiate unexpectedly? Do not limit congeniality to times of scheduled interaction, when you are "on duty." Always be genuinely and thoroughly welcoming.
- Be attentive to key introductions. Are there people in the congregation of the same age or interest who may share a special kinship with the initiate? Are there smaller groups, like church school classes or special-interest groups, that could help break the ice for the initiate?
- Give gifts. A random act of giving highlights the graciousness of God's love. If the initiate does not have a Bible, buy her or him one. Have her or his name printed on the cover. Buy your initiate a hymnal. Are there books you have found particularly helpful for spiritual growth? Consider buying your initiate a copy. Consider giving other gifts—even small ones and not necessarily "spiritual" ones—just for the pleasure of creating joy in another person.
- Be attentive to the childcare needs your initiate may have when attending the formational group sessions. Is there some way you can help meet this need?
- Be willing to provide transportation to meetings required in the formation process. Surprise the initiate one weekend. Even if she or he regularly attends services alone, arrange to take the initiate out to breakfast (or lunch), and go to worship together.
- Sharing fellowship at a meal is one of the simplest, yet most profound biblical gestures of Christian love. Invite her or him to your home for a meal. Take your initiate out to eat. If your church has a regularly scheduled fellowship meal, offer to accompany your initiate.
- Write letters of encouragement to your initiate, and recruit others to do so. A kind word at just the right moment can mean a great deal.
- Introduce your initiate to the great saints of the church. Acquire copies of *For All the Saints: A Calendar of Commemorations for United Methodists,* edited by Clifton F. Guthrie. This book, organized to be read throughout the year, is an anthology of short sketches about great Christians inside and outside of the Methodist tradition. Read it and discuss it with your initiate.

• What are your own ideas on how to be a host?

_____

_____

_____

_____

THE SPONSOR AS LANGUAGE TUTOR

In the first chapter I suggested that it is helpful to see Christianity as a language and to imagine Christian formation (particularly preparing for baptism) as learning to speak the language. I also suggested that like a verbal language, Christianity has a vocabulary and a grammar that define how all of the pieces should fit together. The vocabulary includes the terms and phrases the church uses. This vocabulary should also include the activities that are the essential building blocks for living as a follower of Christ. These activities include worshipping, giving, serving, praying, and studying. Like those who learn a language, mature Christians have learned the rules and relationships by which all of this vocabulary fits together to form a language with meaning (grammar).

But, for those who have yet to be baptized and are not yet fully formed in the way of Christ, that language is not yet known. Some church terms are indecipherable to them. Some Christian activities are in conflict with the values and ways of the world. There can be inexperience in using this vocabulary. And it is not clear at all how the whole thing fits together.

The sponsor must serve as a Christian language tutor for an initiate. A sponsor should provide an opportunity for the initiate to practice what is being learned. In fact, a sponsor should insist upon it. Like a tutor, a sponsor should be in constant dialogue with the initiate so that the initiate is growing in her or his ability to act as a follower of Christ. And, like any good tutor, a sponsor should provide a point of accountability. Any grammar has internal rules that must be followed for the language to make sense and the vocabulary to be useful. Christianity is no different. Private devotion without service to God's world, for instance, is not biblical. The sponsor is the one who can help the initiate practice the grammar of Christian living in the reign of God.

The image of a sponsor as a language tutor also supplements the other ministries and activities of baptismal formation. Worship services provide the basic "classroom" for learning the language of Christianity. The catechesis (the word refers to experiences of listening to God's Word and of being formed in the Christian faith) taking place in formational group sessions provides a sort of "language lab" to learn the dynamics in more detail. And sponsors, as language tutors, provide the practical point of experimenting with what has been learned.

The sponsor's role may sound difficult, but it really is not. Simply put, it is helping the initiate to bring together her or his growing sense of the values and practices of Christ and the realities of the everyday world. I had a wonderful opportunity when I was a Boy Scout to serve as a language tutor for a young boy who had moved to Texas from South America. Much of my job was to take this boy with me as I did normal, American teenager stuff. It was amazing how quickly he learned to speak English just by hanging around with me and my friends. It made the classroom English he was learning come alive. In like manner, a sponsor helps to provide a point of contact with the world to put into practice the Christianity being learned, all with a touch of encouragement and accountability. The goal is to immerse the initiate so deeply in the reign of God that she or he becomes fluent in Christianity, able to speak it without conscious thought.

IDEAS FOR BEING A LANGUAGE TUTOR

- Practice looking at and listening to things from the initiate's perspective. Become aware of the "insider" terminology that a congregation uses. Ask the initiate if there are terms or practices that need interpretation.
- Know intimately what is taking place in the formational group sessions. What activities of walking with Christ are being stressed? Think creatively about how you could give the initiate an opportunity to practice these activities. Be bold. Schedule participation in a mission trip for both of you. Take advantage of opportunities for sacrificial service. Feed the hungry. Take part in Christian political activity.
- Remember the embarrassment that is normal when publicly trying out a new language. Create a sheltered environment in which the initiate can experiment.
- Find a form of Christian music that you both enjoy. Listen to it together, and discuss the words.
- Covenant to read and discuss *Gracious Voices: Shouts & Whispers for God Seekers* together. This volume, part of the Christian Initiation series, is an anthology of passages from a variety of Christian sources, selected and organized to supplement a journey in Christian discipleship.
- Covenant to read and discuss a program of biblical texts together. An excellent possibility is to read the passages found in the church lectionary.
- What are your own ideas on how to be a language tutor?

_____

_____

_____

_____

THE SPONSOR AS EXEMPLAR

Remember the quote from the first chapter about how most people learn the "doing" aspect of being a Christian: "One learns to fast, pray, repent, celebrate, and serve the good of one's neighbors less by being lectured on these matters than by close association with people who do these things with regular ease and flair." A sponsor should be one of the people who follow Christ in specific ways "with regular ease and flair."

The key question for a sponsor as exemplar is this: "How can I exemplify the best aspects of my own Christian walk—and the walks of other mature Christians—without being arrogant about it?" The answer is to show the initiate, as honestly as you can, what it means to walk with Christ. *Demonstration* is the key idea.

Much of an exemplar's influence may be subtle or indirect. Because of this subtlety, it is easy to underestimate the power of an exemplar's presence. But it should not be underestimated.

This power, subtle though it may be, was vividly demonstrated for me when I witnessed a sudden change in the behavior of my young daughter, Charissa. Since she was a very young child, I have tried to get her to say, "Yes, sir" and "No, sir" and "Yes, ma'am" and "No ma'am" when speaking to adults, just as I had learned when I was a boy growing up in Texas. But she was not growing up in Texas. Although she was born there, my family had moved to a different state when she was a young child. All of my desires about the "sir" and "ma'am" business seemed in vain because she had no friends or classmates who used the terms. But an amazing thing happened. In the summer before she started first grade, my family moved back to Texas. Within just a few days of first grade, she was saying "sir" and "ma'am" as if it were second nature.

What made the difference? It was not a change in my influence. My level of instruction as her father had neither increased nor decreased. I believe it was the subtle, yet powerful, influence of example. In the state we had lived previously she had no peer, or exemplar, to model the behavior. In Texas she was surrounded by them. Even without consciously thinking about it, my daughter picked up the prevailing practice of those surrounding her. These young exemplars gave her a standard to imitate, and they did not even know they were doing it!

IDEAS FOR BEING AN EXEMPLAR

- Do you have a special outlet for Christian service? What is your own form of Christian service? Invite and include your charge to participate in this ministry with you.
- Pray with your initiate and for your initiate. Model for her or him how to pray. Demonstrate the Christian concern that underlies intercessory prayer. Invite the initiate to participate in a set period of daily prayer time with you.
- Lead your initiate in times of intercessory prayer for others. Help her or him to reflect on how both of you may be led to help those for whom you have prayed.
- Be regular in your own attendance at worship services and other important church activities. Model a high level of commitment. Offer to help your charge overcome difficulties in establishing her or his own attendance patterns.
- Without being phony or contrived, do not hesitate to show your joy in being a Christian, following Christ, and participating in the life of the church.
- What are your own ideas on how to be an exemplar?

_____

_____

_____

_____

THE SPONSOR AS MENTOR

In the book, *Connecting: The Mentoring Relationships You Need to Succeed in Life*, authors Paul D. Stanley and J. Robert Clinton discuss a variety of roles that mentors can play. Among these roles, Stanley and Clinton explore the nature of a mentor as a sponsor, defining sponsorship as a relational process in which a mentor having credibility and positional or spiritual authority within an organization or network relates to a mentoree not having those resources. The mentor enables the development of the mentoree and the mentoree's influence in the organization.[15]

Although *Connecting* focuses mainly on sponsorial mentoring in businesses or other large organizations, its concept can generate ideas for baptismal sponsors.

As suggested in Stanley's and Clinton's description of mentors, three aspects of a sponsor's role in this regard stand out. First, a mentor should be attentive to the person under her or his charge. The mentoree should remain central in the mentor's attention and thinking. Second, a mentor should have an aim for the mentoree. The basis of the relationship should be goal-oriented for the benefit of the mentoree. Third, as Stanley and Clinton put it, a mentor should have a "sense of destiny" for the mentoree, a vision of what that person can become.[16]

For a baptismal sponsor, these notions serve as reminders of the initiate's potential. A sponsor should think about and pray for the initiate. Expect God to inspire your musing about the well-being of your charge. A sponsor should be mindful of the gifts and graces that God is manifesting in the initiate. Aspirations about having the initiate find her or his proper place in the church's ministry is the natural fruit.

IDEAS FOR BEING A MENTOR

- Set up regular times to pray and think about your charge. Keep this relationship at the center of your daily life.
- Ask God to share with you God's own aspirations for this person.
- Review the lists of spiritual gifts in the Bible (Romans 12:3-8; 1 Corinthians 12:4-11; Ephesians 4:7-13). Try to discern what capabilities God has granted your initiate for the benefit of the church and for service to the world. Consider opportunities for exercising these gifts in the congregation.
- What are your own ideas on how to be a mentor?

_____

_____

_____

_____

THE SPONSOR AS GODPARENT

The image of sponsors as godparents is an ancient one. Indeed, the term "godparent" is one of the earliest synonyms for "sponsor." In fact, through church history the term "godparent" has been preferred over "sponsor," which is considered more generic. Today, many people have strong sentimental associations about what it means to be a godparent, sometimes including assumptions about taking on the responsibility of raising the baptized children if the parents were unable.

Originally, the term "godparent" was used in a more general sense, one that applied to sponsors for both adults and children. Moreover, in early references, the term was a natural metaphor, based on the broad responsibilities assumed by all baptismal sponsors. In one early reference, to be quoted at length in Chapter Six, an ancient preacher said that sponsors could be considered as parents because they encourage, counsel, and correct those for whom they have responsibility. According to this preacher, sponsors could be considered god- or spiritual-parents because they are to instruct their "children"—adults and babies alike—with great affection.

It is this ancient, more general sense of the term that fits our image of baptismal sponsors. There are two aspects to this image. The first involves generation: As parents bring children into the world, sponsors help newborn Christians develop. The second includes ongoing, well-rounded nurturing that a parent extends to a child. To paraphrase the ancient preacher: Sponsors as godparents must provide strong guidance, tempered with great affection. These two aspects make the image of a godparent appropriate for all sponsors.

A more modern, and more specific, use of the term "godparent" also must be acknowledged. This use of the term differentiates between sponsors and godparents; it is this latter use of the term that you will find in the Christian Initiation series. Perhaps a word of explanation would be helpful, particularly in the instance of children's initiation, when godparents are more likely to be chosen.

In the case of the baptism of children, there are actually three parties who exercise sponsorial responsibilities. First, we must be quite clear that parents are the *primary* sponsors ("parental sponsors") for their own children. Parents have the main responsibility for forming their children in the way of Christ. Others assist them. Second, there are the "regular sponsors," perhaps best called *congregational* or *church* sponsors. These are the representatives of the congregation, assisting parents in the preparation for their children's baptism by fulfilling the roles described throughout this book. If the parents are unbaptized inquirers, these congregational or church sponsors should also sponsor the parents in their formation. Finally, there may also be *godparents*. Godparents fulfill a role similar to church sponsors, except that they may exercise a lifelong spiritual relationship with the baptized. In contrast to church sponsors, godparents need not be members of the denomination or local congregation, but they should be active Christians in their own church. They should be chosen after consulting with the pastor or catechist. Thus, at the service of baptism itself, a child may have both sponsors and godparents. (Note that because the service for baptism does not make reference to godparents, some planning must be given to determining their role in the service.) Differentiating between sponsors and godparents allows parents to include people as godparents who may not otherwise qualify as sponsors.

IDEAS FOR BEING A GODPARENT

- Perhaps the importance of a godparent image is the emphasis on real affection. Consider how you could appropriately show affection to your initiate.
- For those who are asked to sponsor children, read *The Godparent Book* by Elaine Ramshaw. It is full of useful ideas.
- Find a creative way to help your charge remember the anniversary of her or his baptism.
- What are your own ideas on how to be a godparent?

_____

_____

_____

_____

QUESTIONS FOR REFLECTION

❧ Which of the different images of the sponsor as presenter to the initiate do you think is the most important?

❧ Based on how initiation formation is handled in your church, what adjustments would you make to this chapter's description of the role of sponsors as presenters of God's grace?

❧ Think about the different images in this chapter, the nature of initiation formation in your congregation, and, especially, the person you sponsor. Developing a plan of action, how could you best present the grace of God to your charge?

THE SPONSOR'S ROLE OF PRESENTING THE CANDIDATE AS GRACED INDIVIDUAL

"I PRESENT": A SPONSOR'S BASIC MINISTRY TO THE CHURCH

"I present...." These words are a sponsor's first publicly spoken words. They come in the first service for the initiation of adults, "A Service for Welcoming Hearers." Indeed, other than the initial extemporaneous greeting by the pastor and the catechist, they are the first words spoken in the church about signaling the initiation process. The first public act of a sponsor is to say, "I present *(name)*, who desires to learn the way of Christ."[17]

The importance of this simple utterance should not be underestimated. The ability to say this phrase with integrity should reflect a sponsor's familiarity with the initiate. This public presentation should be seen as symbolic of the sponsor's accompanying the initiate on the baptismal journey. This is one of the basic ministries for a sponsor, condensed and expressed in the two simple words, "I present."

The service of baptism also begins in this way. A sponsor stands before the church (the instructions call only for a "representative of the congregation," but the role is most naturally a sponsor's), utters the same words "I present," and then names the individual. As discussed in Chapter Two, the sponsor's ministry of presentation *from* the candidate *to* the church is fundamental.

One reason that this act of presentation is so important is because the church depends on a sponsor to attest to the integrity of the initiate's formation in Christ at crucial moments in worship. To avoid any "hint of mere formality" (as *Come to the Waters* puts it) the church relies upon the soundness of the presentation of and witness on behalf of an initiate. Although the discernment process is a cooperative effort (as we will see later), it is the sponsor upon whom this public responsibility of presentation falls.

The weight that the church attaches to the responsibility of the sponsor to make a true and fair presentation of the candidate is not a recent phenomenon. As we will see in the last chapter, many of the earliest discussions about the ministry of sponsors highlight just how much the church depended, even then, on sponsors. Some of the images may seem a little strong. One early preacher, for example, likened a sponsor's witness for and presentation of an initiate to co-signing a note where the sponsor becomes indebted to God. Despite its intensity, this image still contains a helpful truth for us today: Formation for initiation is a joint endeavor, with sponsors playing a particularly crucial public role in preserving the integrity of the process. Although the words spoken may be few, a sponsor's presentation of an initiate to the church during worship is a crucial act.

As we saw in Chapter Two, a sponsor presents the initiate to the congregation in two ways during the worship services. First, a sponsor physically accompanies his or her initiate. Second, a sponsor verbally presents the initiate, names the initiate, and attests to the initiate's readiness to proceed.

Both presentations during worship should be paralleled by a sponsor's ministry outside of worship. A sponsor must prepare for the presentations during the worship services by participating in ministries outside of them. In the rest of the chapter, I offer some key images to help you prepare the initiate for presentation to the congregation.

THE SPONSOR AS COMPANION

The journey toward Christ in the process of initiation should not be a lonely one. As the title of this book declares, sponsors accompany those who are on the journey toward Christ and toward the reign of God. Two sets of footprints, not one, should be left on the path that leads toward Jesus Christ.

This aspect of a sponsor's ministry can be called companionship. The word "companionship" connotes the idea of sharing bread with another person. This idea hints at the nature of a sponsor's ministry. The goal is not just eating the same kind of food—we do that often enough when we eat with friends at a fast food restaurant—but sharing the basic necessities of Christian fellowship. It suggests getting to know someone as a fellow follower of Christ and becoming joined in common concerns and viewpoints. Sponsors must know their charges in Christian fellowship. Companionship means coming to a point where you, the sponsor, can see things from the initiate's viewpoint. This companionship means that initiates make the journey toward baptism with someone who is empathetic.

The sponsor's act of presenting the initiate in the worship services presumes this intimacy. When the sponsor names the individual at his or her side during a worship service, the congregation assumes that the sponsor knows the individual. The presentation should be more than reciting a name; it should be considered as an introduction of a friend.

The image of companion can be defined further with the help of a related image: the sponsor as a fellow pilgrim. This image has several important components. First, it highlights the progressive nature of being a Christian; walking with Christ involves movement toward the goal of growing in faith and in the enjoyment of God. Being a Christian is a pilgrimage. Sponsors are, as *Come to the Waters* suggests, people "who walk with others during the stages of Christian initiation."[18]

At times, perhaps, there will only be one set of footprints because the initiate will need to learn the walk by stepping in the footprints of the sponsor. One of the gifts a sponsor has to share is prior knowledge of some aspects of the walk. This knowledge is gained by having a head start in the pilgrimage. It is not superiority that a sensitive sponsor offers in the Christian pilgrimage; it is prior experience.

At times during the pilgrimage, the sponsor will walk at the initiate's side. At other times the sponsor will move ahead, motioning and encouraging the initiate to move forward and enjoy God more fully.

IDEAS FOR BEING A COMPANION

- Learn the full name of your charge. Is there a special family significance in the name? Is it a biblical name, or does it have some special religious significance? Do you know your initiate's nickname? After consulting both the initiate and the pastor, know the name by which you will present your charge in the worship services.
- At some point, ask your initiate the following question: If he or she could pick a new name, what would it be? It is customary in some Christian traditions to pick a new name, particularly that of a saint or biblical character. This is not necessarily suggested here, but it can be a helpful exercise to find out with whom the initiate identifies himself or herself.
- Always be ready to name and introduce your charge in church settings. Take the initiative to make sure that the initiate becomes properly known.
- Do not be afraid to be an advocate for your initiate's concerns and questions during the formation process. Give his or her concerns a voice.
- Listen to and learn the personal story of your initiate. Look for the appropriate moment to share this information. What has brought him or her to this point? What are the specifics of his or her pilgrimage?
- Reflect on the pitfalls and highlights of your own Christian pilgrimage. Be sensitive to the same in the journey of your charge.
- What are your own ideas on how to be a companion or a fellow pilgrim?

_____

_____

_____

_____

THE SPONSOR AS WITNESS

We noted in Chapter One that the process of formation for Christian initiation is a rhythm of stages marked by certain thresholds. Chapter Two showed the thresholds to be worship services in which sponsors typically play an important role.

Particularly crucial in these services are the occasions when a sponsor is called upon to witness to the readiness of an initiate. This is one of the most important, and most classic, of a sponsor's presentation responsibilities. Foremost among these occasions is the "Affirmation by Sponsors" in the service for calling persons to baptism. (This service normally takes place on the first Sunday of Lent and starts the period of intensive preparation.) Because this part of the service is so pivotal, it will be reproduced here in its entirety:

The pastor, speaking to the sponsors, says:
Dear brothers and sisters, as sponsors and friends of _____ (*names of hearers*), you
    know that *they* seek initiation into Christ's holy church.
We want to know that *they* are prepared to enter life in Christ.
You have walked with *them* on a journey of conversion.
You have prayed for *them* to know and to heed the voice of Christ.
You have witnessed *their* love of God and of neighbor in daily living.
As God is your witness, tell us of *their* readiness
to obey Christ's call to life in the baptismal covenant.

Have they faithfully joined in the worship of God?
    They have.
Have they heard God's word and followed Jesus in their daily life?
    They have.
Have they come to know Christ's story and way, and *have they* engaged in ministry
with the poor and the neglected?
    They have.

*Here each sponsor may speak in a brief and focused way of the hearers' growth and
courage in learning the Christian life. The affirmation should be expressed in words
that witness to God's gracious work in the hearers' hearts, minds, and actions. Each
sponsor's witness should express God's love and should neither praise the hearers nor
expose or embarrass them.*[19]

The service for calling children to baptism through their parents is very similar.
Each service continues with the congregation making a renewed statement of support to the hearer, based upon the sponsor's witness.

The importance of the sponsor's witness to the congregation on behalf of the
hearer cannot be overemphasized. This act of witness is the culmination of a long
period of formation preceding this moment, and it is the catalyst for the immediate
preparation for baptism. The words of the service reinforce the solemn nature of the
witness: "As God is your witness...." To avoid "any hint of mere formality," the sponsor's witness in the worship service must be preceded by "[a]ppropriate face-to-face
conferences and discernment of readiness by those who have worked with the candidates." These conferences and discernment of readiness should obviously include
the sponsor.[20]

Because the witness on the initiate's behalf is such a fundamental ministry for
sponsors, it is appropriate to give some consideration to the important process of *discernment*. The responsibility for discernment is not solely left to the sponsor. The
pastor, the catechist, and others who have worked with the initiates are also responsible. Even the initiate is responsible! Indeed, good discernment procedures are
opportunities for honest self-reflection by the initiate.

The method of discernment can vary, depending on the particular circumstances
in the congregation. Most methods will involve direct conferences between the initiate and those responsible for discernment. Face-to-face conferences should not be
considered as a "test" that the initiate must pass before moving on in the process.
The goal of an initiate's formation is not just learning to recite church facts or beliefs

or attaining a high level of church attendance, but conforming the initiate's life to Christ; a conformation that involves every dimension of the person's life. Because the goal is so encompassing, a face-to-face "examination" does not conclusively reveal whether the goal has been reached.

A sponsor's observation of the initiate's progress in formation, particularly outside the formational group sessions or the face-to-face conferences, is a crucial element in the process. *Come to the Waters* calls explicitly for that sort of knowledge in its description of the role of a sponsor:

> For adults preparing for baptism or reaffirmation of baptism, sponsors know or get to know them so well that they can vouch for the conversion and sincere intention of each to live as a disciple of Christ.[21]

A sponsor preserves the integrity of the discernment process by bringing this kind of knowledge to the discussion.

Because they are called upon to provide public witness before the congregation on behalf of initiates, sponsors can be neither uninvolved nor at odds with the general process used to discern the initiates' readiness. Although the discernment process involves the pastor, the catechists, and the initiates, the sponsors' role is somewhat unique because of their particular worship responsibilities. Ideally, everyone involved in the discernment process will agree about the readiness of an initiate. However, because the sponsor alone bears *public* witness, he or she must be comfortable with the conclusion. With the weight of a public witness looming, a sponsor has a special role in insisting upon integrity and truth in the discernment process.

Whatever the method for arranging both ongoing discernment and face-to-face conferences, it is absolutely vital that the criteria for discernment be clearly defined. Simply put, the congregation and its leaders must clarify what they expect to find in those progressing in the way of Christ. This clarity is especially important for sponsors since they are the ones who must publicly witness to the progress. As a pastor, I have found it fruitful to seek, with the leaders involved, this clarity at the very beginning of the process of Christian initiation. Seeking an answer to the question "What are the basic characteristics of a Christian?" (and similar questions) not only gave us guidelines as to how to develop the formational group sessions but reawakened some spiritual sensitivities in the leaders themselves.

The criteria for discernment should be rooted in the structure and nature of the process of initiation itself. Remember that there are several stages in the journey of formation, each with their own issues. Thus, discernment should focus on the readiness of the initiate to deal with the issues raised at each stage. Appropriate questions may be asked at the thresholds between stages. (See the different questions and issues appropriate for each threshold in *Come to the Waters*, pp. 33-35, 101-103.)

Discernment is especially needful at the threshold between the formation and intensive preparation stages. Here sponsors must carefully consider the questions they are to answer in the service for calling persons to baptism. Sponsors need to be clear about what they consider reasonable expectations for the candidate and about the church's expectations on these same matters. These questions, as quoted from *Come to the Waters* (p. 114), reflect a balanced, broad possibility for the hoped-for formation:

> *Have they* [the initiates] faithfully joined in the worship of God?
> *Have they* heard God's word and followed Jesus in their daily life?
> *Have they* come to know Christ's story and way, and *have they* engaged in ministry with the poor and the neglected?

Note that the initial question is about having joined in the worship of God. The intent is to inquire about more than just regular attendance, although that matter is important too. The next two questions deal with the "knowledge" being gained. The concern in these questions does not relate to knowing facts and dates but to knowing Christ, which affects the initiate's daily living. That is why these questions have two parts: The first deals with the knowledge of the heart, and the second focuses on how it is being lived out. The question about having heard God's Word is complemented by an inquiry about whether the candidate has followed Jesus in daily life. The question about whether the candidate has come to know "Christ's story and way" is coupled with an inquiry about whether the candidate has ministered to the "poor and the neglected."

A sponsor must also be aware of the catechesis provided in the formational group sessions. Sponsors should attend all of the group sessions, so their participation in the catechesis assures this knowledge. At a minimum, sponsors should be aware of the different areas covered in the sessions, typically including Scripture, worship, prayer and spiritual disciplines, the creed, and ministry in daily life. Remember that the goal is a transformed life rather than scholarship in biblical or church facts.

It takes courage to be truly discerning in these matters. It is not easy. Many people feel that baptism is a service that should be performed by the church on demand. Such people will make their displeasure known—sometimes to district superintendents and bishops—if their consumer sensibilities are thwarted. "What is there to discern?" eager parents and grandparents may ask. Furthermore, some may demand, "We want our baby baptized." Others approach baptism with a variety of other goals in place, like a desire to sate the hounding of a family member. They may find it hard to understand why the church will not help them if a decision is made that the candidate is not ready for baptism. All of these dynamics make the process of discernment difficult.

I speak from personal pastoral experience, having both failed and succeeded in exercising this discernment. Sometimes I have wondered if I did the correct thing. One instance, in particular, still haunts me. The sponsor and I were concerned about a teenage candidate in our church's catechumenate. She was minimally responsive and attentive in and outside of our formational sessions. She showed little evidence of any spiritual fire or interest. Many times I could not help but think that she had enrolled as a hearer merely to satisfy her mother's desires. To complicate the matter, this candidate had a younger sister in the same catechumenate who was making excellent progress in being formed as a disciple for Christ. Furthermore, the teenage catechumens were the next generation in several lines of generations from this family in this church. Everyone expected that the sisters would be baptized; and the mother did not seem to be the kind of person who would like to be told "no." The sponsor and I prayed and talked. We decided to baptize the teenager and hope for the best. But I felt uncomfortable with the decision and feel the same to this day. I do not believe that we did what was in the best interest of the girl and the church.

Even when discernment is done appropriately, it can still be a difficult decision. Once two adults asked me to baptize them. After talking with them, it was quite clear that they had no intention of being involved with the church, the body of Christ. There simply was no communal aspect to their desire to be baptized into Christ. After several conversations and much prayer, I decided not to baptize them. It was difficult to tell them of my decision, although they accepted it when I explained my thinking in detail.

It is perhaps best if a decision that a candidate is *not* ready for the next stage comes through a mutual discernment process in which the candidate shares. Indeed, the goal of the discernment process is not to make heavy-handed, unilateral decisions. Rather it is to guide the candidate to a conscious awareness of his or her own readiness. This goal is particularly true in any face-to-face conferences held for discernment. (None of this should imply that the leaders involved should not be clear on the criteria for discernment, as discussed above.)

Whenever face-to-face conferences with candidates are used as a part of the discernment process, one Christian educator has suggested that a good way of involving candidates in mutual discernment entails asking them questions in a four-fold process of apprehension, appraisal, affirmation, and application.[22] This method can be used during face-to-face conferences that may precede any of the worship services marking transitions from one stage to the next. It may also be used during any of the stages. (See *Come to the Waters*, pp. 103-108, for a discussion of these stages and services.)

The four-fold method described here should not be confused with the basic rhythm of the initiation process outlined in the section "How the Process of Initiation Works" in Chapter One. Rather, this method provides one possibility for how the *internal order* of face-to-face discernment conferences may be structured. Such conferences may occur several times at any or all of the stages of Christian initiation (inquiry, formation, intensive preparation, and integration).

In this four-fold method, sponsors and others may use the four worship services outlined in *Come to the Waters* (pp. 109-121) to derive questions with which to lead initiates through an increasing awareness of the depth of commitment called for in a particular service and the breadth of the loving commitment that God makes as well. Thus, in the first phase of the four-fold method, initiates are led to *apprehend* the basic substance of the service through questions such as "How is this service like a covenant?"; "What does it mean to make a covenant?"; "Who are the parties to this covenant?"; and "Is there a particular phrase or aspect that caught your attention?" In the second phase initiates are asked questions to help them *appraise* the substance of the service at a deeper level: "What was it about this phrase or aspect that caught your attention?"; "What images or situations come to your mind when you think of those particular phrases or aspects?"; "Which parts of the service evoke positive or negative feelings?"; "What images or situations come to mind when you hear these words?"; "What does it mean for you to make this covenant?"; and "What does it mean for the other parties to make this covenant?"

The questions of the first two phases of the four-fold method lead to the final sets of questions that outline a more serious discernment of readiness. *Affirmation* is phase three. Here the initiate is asked to identify areas he or she can or cannot affirm in the service. Appropriate questions could include: "Which sections of the service do you have a problem believing to be true?"; "Can you give reasons?"; "Which sections do you believe to truly state your personal beliefs?"; and "Why do you believe these statements true?" The final phase involves asking questions *applying* the commitment made: "If you go through this service and make its covenant, do you see it changing your relationships (a) at work or school, (b) with your spouse, (c) with your children or family members, (d) with neighbors and friends, (e) in your use of wealth, time, and energy, (f) when you read the newspaper and listen to the news?"; "How will it change your relationships in these areas?"; and "How do you anticipate living out this commitment and growing into it?"

It is hoped that these questions will give the initiate, the sponsor, and any other participants a greater insight of an initiate's readiness and his or her intentions. Based on the initiate's answers, mutual discernment should be possible. Be direct; ask the initiate whether he or she is ready for baptism.

Of course, these questions are not the only ones that could be asked. For instance, *Come to the Waters* suggests the following questions as especially appropriate in the period of intensive preparation before baptism: "What must change (die) in you in order that Christ's reign of love and justice may flourish in your life?"; "How will you live for Jesus in your daily life?"; and "What desires and affections need realignment for you to follow Christ with your whole heart?"[23]

Regardless of the particular questions asked, a sponsor must provide an accurate witness for the initiate during the discernment process. A sponsor must always have that goal in mind.

IDEAS FOR BEING A WITNESS

- Read through the appropriate worship services for your initiate on a regular basis. Immerse yourself in their language. Reflect on what is being asked of the initiate and on the implicit promises of God. There is no substitute for familiarity with the services.
- Pray for yourself and for the others involved in discernment. Ask for a bold combination of gentleness, insightfulness, and courage.
- Make sure you understand the particulars of your initiate's journey. What are reasonable expectations, given his or her particular situation and background? People should be held accountable for the light they have received, not the light they have not received. Keep in mind that discipleship is about grace and about being faithful in practicing the means of grace.

- If your church invites you to provide a brief witness (in addition to responding to the questions that are part of the worship service), think carefully about what you will say. Remember that this witness about the initiate is also a witness about the goodness of God's character and activity. What can you say that will edify the church in this manner? Remember that the goal is neither to praise nor embarrass the initiate.
- What are your own ideas on how to be a witness?

_____

_____

_____

_____

QUESTIONS FOR REFLECTION

❧ What makes the analogy of a journey, or pilgrimage, a useful image for understanding the nature of a Christian life? Do you think it is a biblical one?

❧ This chapter suggests that courage is required for truthfully establishing discernment. Do you agree? Why or why not?

❧ Do you think the church has the responsibility to tell some people "no" when they request baptism? What are those situations?

❧ Why do you think the church requires a sponsor to witness to the hearer's readiness before the stage of intensive preparation begins?

❧ How could providing witnesses or testimonies be edifying to the church?

Chapter Five

Practical Considerations

Selecting Sponsors

How should sponsors be selected? The question is not as easy as it seems. Several means of connecting sponsors with initiates are possible, each having advantages and disadvantages. Let us review some of the basic choices.

1. Let the Initiate Select the Sponsor

One obvious method is to allow the one preparing for baptism or the parents of the child to be baptized to select the sponsor. This approach is the one I have used in my pastoral ministry. It has worked reasonably well in the churches I have served.

The clear advantage is that the parties involved already have an existing relationship. Usually the inquirer's or parents' comfort level is high because the sponsor is already known as a trusted friend. The sponsor usually already knows helpful information about the background of her or his charge and the nature of the charge's spiritual journey.

This familiarity can also be a disadvantage, however. A prior friendship or relationship could make it difficult for the sponsor to exercise some of her or his responsibilities, particularly those associated with holding the charge accountable for growth in the Christian faith. If the initiate's original selection was based on sentimental reasons, or if the sponsor is afraid to jeopardize a longtime friendship, it would be very easy for a sponsor to overlook the more difficult aspects of her or his responsibilities. This is the reason why I have never allowed family members to be considered for or selected as sponsors. I keep this rule even in the cases of the baptism of children, and I believe it has been a wise decision.

Similarly, inquirers may choose sponsors who will not be faithful to their responsibilities. They may propose a sponsor who has little or no relationship with the local congregation. Intervention by the pastor can be awkward. Recently, for example, in one of my churches a young girl preparing for baptism wanted to select a school teacher as her sponsor. While the teacher was a member of the local church, she had been inactive during my tenure. Consequently, I did not feel that the teacher could model an adequate level of involvement for this candidate. I directed the girl to make another choice, and she chose a sponsor who was very involved as an integral member of the church.

One of the basic qualifications for being a sponsor is a level of maturity in walking in the Christian faith. Active involvement in a local church is, I believe, one of the ways Christian maturity is reflected. At times, an inquirer may suggest a sponsor who is not a Christian or one who is not active in a local congregation. How can the sponsor fulfill her or his representative role for the church in that scenario? For this reason, I prefer that sponsors for children be chosen from the active membership of the church in which the child will be raised.

2. TRAIN A GROUP OF SPONSORS

Another method for selecting sponsors, which perhaps avoids some of the pitfalls but still allows the inquirer some discretion, is to have an already trained group of sponsors from which the inquirers can select.

This idea came to me in a previous pastorate. After several years I began to notice that the same people were selected repeatedly as sponsors, even when the inquirers were making the choices. I began to think about organizing these people, along with other capable members, into an "order" of sponsors. This approach has several advantages: It allows for more intentional, intensive sponsor training; it ensures that every inquirer has a sponsor fully aware of her or his responsibilities; and it enables sponsors over time to grow more familiar and comfortable in the role.

Furthermore, I began to notice that the inquirers' experiences outside the formational group sessions were extremely crucial in their acclimatization in the Christian faith and their initiation in the reign of God. In fact, much, if not most, of the real formation took place outside the catechesis. Consequently, I began to dream about extending the period of formal preparation from nine months to two years. In the new scheme a short period of catechesis (four to six weeks) on specific issues would alternate with intensive work between the initiate and the sponsor outside the session setting. Obviously, a predetermined, well-trained group of sponsors would be necessary to make this plan work.

There are some disadvantages to this method. If the same sponsors are "recycled," what are the effects on long-term relationships between sponsors and their charges? The responsibility of a sponsor does not end at the moment of baptism. How many people could someone sponsor before the weight of continuing responsibility became overwhelming? Similarly, there is the question about a shortage of sponsors. What should a church do if the number of inquirers exceeds the number of available sponsors? And there is always the question of relationship: What if the relationship between the initiate and the sponsor does not work? What guidelines should be given to the inquirer to help her or him in selecting a sponsor?

3. ALLOW THE INITIATE MORE THAN ONE SPONSOR

Another possible method in selecting and assigning sponsors is to use a mixed system. A candidate could have dual sponsors who fulfill different roles: one who rigorously represents the church in Christian formation and one who is selected for more sentimental reasons. Or, a candidate could have different sponsors for different stages of the initiation process: At one stage a church-assigned sponsor is used, and at another stage a sponsor selected on the basis of close friendship takes over. In one denomination, for example, instructions for the services regularly call for one sponsor to guide the initiate up to the first service in Lent, when the initiate's readiness for baptism is affirmed. Instead of the first sponsor making this affirmation, however, another sponsor—called a "godparent"—who has a close friendship with the initiate assumes the sponsor's public responsibilities from this point forward.

In some ways using a mixed method would seem to offer the best of all worlds. But some caution must be exercised. For instance, a church should be careful about when the sponsorial switch is made (a potential problem in the previous example). The public affirmation of the hearer's readiness for baptism is one of the most important acts performed by a sponsor and must be based on actual familiarity with the hearer's progress in the faith. In light of this solemnity, it is best if the affirmation is made by the sponsor who has accompanied the initiate throughout the formation process. This is especially true if the new sponsor is chosen by the initiate for sentimental reasons.

This possible conflict between a sponsor's integrity and sentimentality seems most acute in cases of a sponsor/godparent selected by a family preparing for the baptism of a child. Sentimentally-selected sponsors have their rightful place, but church-assigned sponsors have the objectivity needed to answer honestly the questions regarding "[the initiate's] readiness to obey Christ's call in the baptismal covenant."[24]

Note that *Come to the Waters* (p. 124) makes a distinction between sponsors and godparents for children. The guidelines suggested there should be followed. At a minimum, sponsors should be baptized Christians who are members of the congregation in which the baptism will occur; godparents must be professing Christians, but they do not have to be members of the congregation. The selection of sponsors and godparents should be made after a consultation with the pastor or catechist.

If greater emphasis on the objectivity of sponsors is sought, a congregation should consider assigning sponsors with no input from the initiate. This method ensures that sponsors are baptized members and are selected in consultation with the pastor or the catechist. However, assigning sponsors is potentially risky: The all-important rapport may be missing in a created initiate/sponsor match. Of course, this potential issue could be a topic to address in the training for sponsors.

Finally, the person instrumental in bringing the initiate to the Christian faith should be considered as a potential sponsor, which is the traditional way for arranging sponsorships. (See the discussion of the early history of sponsors in the next chapter.) How rewarding it is for the initiate and the sponsor to share in the culminating experience of baptism.

QUALITIES AND CRITERIA FOR SPONSORS

When choosing sponsors, one should look for certain desirable qualities. Most are obvious from the nature of the role sponsors play. Consider these:

1. KNOWLEDGE OF THE CHRISTIAN FAITH

It is necessary that a sponsor be a baptized person who upholds the Christian faith. Generally this quality is essential because some of the critical formation for the initiate should come through imitating the sponsor. A sponsor must be able to model basic faith in Christ. Specifically, this faithfulness is required for the sponsor to perform certain duties. In the case of adult candidates, the sponsor will be called upon at the beginning of the period of intensive preparation to attest to the candidate's readiness. Although all harsh judgment and self-righteousness is to be avoided, a sponsor must know the Christian faith to make this decision. In the case of children brought for baptism, the instructions in the service call for sponsors to guide the baptized through both *teaching* and *example* to an acceptance of God's grace and to a profession of faith. To teach and to lead by example, sponsors need sound knowledge of the Christian faith.

2. MATURITY IN THE CHRISTIAN FAITH

Another important quality is maturity in the faith. This does not necessarily refer to a chronological age but to a certain "settledness" in the way of Christ. As another author has noted, newly baptized or newly received members may not be the best candidates for sponsors.[25] Although they may bring great zeal—a desirable quality— they sometimes lack the fully developed perspective that comes from following Christ over a period of time.

3. COMMITMENT TO THE WORK OF THE CHURCH

Sponsors must be able to model committed involvement in a local church. Although this aspect may not sound very "spiritual" and may seem obvious, it is still important. Initiates must be able to see in their sponsors something of the goal to which they themselves aspire. For active sponsors, involvement with initiates seems like a natural outgrowth of prior work in the church; one naturally flows from the other. For sponsors who have come from the margins of church life, involvement does not seem nearly as natural. Perhaps this observation is just my own pastoral perspective, but I believe as the excitement builds toward the moment of baptism, it is most natural for sponsors to see their own high commitment bear fruit in the lives of their charges.

4. WELL-ROUNDEDNESS

Well-roundedness is another desirable quality in sponsors of mature Christian faith. Again, it is hoped that this trait can be transferred to the initiates. The formation initiates receive is intended to shape every aspect of their lives. The goal is formation in the way of God's reign, a reign so comprehensive that no area of the initiate's life should remain untouched by her or his desire to follow Christ. A sponsor should be able to model this quality. Although God's grace finds fruition in lives through a variety of ways, a sponsor should know what it means to be a Christian in the different aspects of life. A sponsor should be able to pray and serve, to worship and guide, to do justice and think about Christian truth.

And it is important that the fruit of God's reign be apparent in the lives of the sponsors. Sponsors should exemplify the inner qualities that the Bible calls the "fruit of the Spirit": love, joy, peace, patience, kindness, generosity, faithfulness, gentleness, and self-control (Galatians 5:22-23a). The presentational role of sponsors is enhanced by the degree with which they are able to walk in the Holy Spirit. Sponsors represent not only the church as a human institution but also the church as a window to the reign of God and the nature of Christ.

5. THE ABILITY TO BUILD RELATIONSHIPS

Relational and interpersonal skills are also very desirable in sponsors. Since a sponsor's formative role does not take place in a large setting but mainly through one-on-one contact, a sponsor should be able to develop lines of communication and to build a relationship with the initiate.

Other material on sponsorship explores in more depth some of the qualities mentioned above. According to an Episcopalian assessment by John Westerhoff entitled "Characteristics of a Helpful Sponsor," useful sponsors

- are able to share intimately and to risk vulnerability; are able to tell of their own pain and sorrow.
- believe God is present and active in the lives of all people, not that one "has it" and another does not; rather some have not yet named God's presence and activities in their lives.
- are affirming persons who can see the image of God in every human being.
- are communal persons who do not see themselves as other than part of a community; that is, they are those who save souls for Christ and for the church.
- do not see the world as being split between the physical and the spiritual, between the rational and the instinctive.
- feel good about themselves as:
  first, children of God and members of the human family;
  second, members of Christ;
  third, members of the Anglican Communion;
  fourth, members of a particular congregation.
- cannot be shocked and are willing to know both the violence in themselves and their reliance on God.
- are clear about their convictions and can name them, but do not need to have others accept them.
- have varied experiences in their lives as Christians and can tell stories about these experiences.
- have a love/hate relationship with the church and can be honest about it.
- are caring and hospitable; they can give people what they want rather than what they need, yet can confront others when confrontation is needed.[26]

This list is helpful for United Methodist sponsors, although the reference to "Anglican Communion" should be substituted with a reference to United Methodism.

Perhaps consideration of all the desirable qualities and the awesomeness of the task to which she or he is called can lead a sponsor to some despair. That is natural, but sponsors need to realize that they cannot be "superwomen" or "supermen." The glory and wonder of God's grace is that it works through us, even in our imperfect state. Indeed this combination of God's grace in our weakness is part of the power of being a sponsor. As previously discussed, a sponsor needs to be recognizable by the initiate as a peer—someone who is like her or him. Yet, the grace of God is seen in the life of the sponsor. That should be the sponsor's constant prayer.

A touch of despair is perhaps inevitable in good sponsorial candidates. One of the qualities of true Christian spirituality is humility. Good prospects naturally assume that they cannot do the job. But that perception is not necessarily true. Humility is an open window through which God can work.

Indeed, humility can be a mark that someone is called to the ministry of sponsorship. One wise, early Methodist noted that a mark of a true calling to a ministry is "when, even though satisfied of duty, there is a self-distrust for the work."[27] In other words, someone can feel the call to ministry but doubt her or his strength to fulfill it. Of course, with the strength of God's grace, you can fulfill this calling.

FORMING AND PREPARING SPONSORS

After their selection, sponsors—particularly new ones—should receive orientation and training for their role. Although there are some parallels to other church experiences and although some tasks will be natural to well-chosen sponsors, some basic preparation is helpful and necessary.

Let us now focus on suggestions about how to accomplish this formation. Of course, these suggestions can be adapted, expanded, or abbreviated to fit your situation.

Sponsor preparation should include three components: direct guidance, private journaling and reflection, and readings coordinated among the sponsors. The manner used to develop these components will differ according to the size of the catechumenate. In a larger catechumenate—where many are preparing for baptism at the same time—there will probably be a need for more structure, both in the catechesis of initiates and the preparation of their sponsors. Thus, when a large group is preparing for baptism simultaneously, a church is likely to have a well-defined place and schedule for catechesis. Preparation of a larger number of sponsors should probably be done in group settings, following a more detailed schedule. In a smaller catechumenate, there is more opportunity to handle things on an *ad hoc* basis, customizing the process for the few people involved.

As to direct guidance, at least one orientation session should be held before or at the onset of sponsors' work with their charges. In a large catechumenate, this session should come before the formal catechesis begins. This initial orientation will steer the sponsors in a common direction by sharing the basic understanding of baptism that underlies the catechumenal process. One possibility is to structure this orientation according to chapter topics in this book: Starting with an understanding of baptism as a process of initiation, sponsors review their worship responsibilities and then look at these activities from the perspectives of being presenters to the initiates on the church's behalf and presenters to the church on the initiates' behalf.

The other goal in this initial orientation is to equip sponsors with needed basic tools. Foremost among these tools will be the skills to build rapport and a caring relationship between sponsor and initiate. A review of good communication skills is essential. Some of the other handbooks written to assist sponsors are very helpful in examining this sort of information. See especially Chapter Five of *Walking Together in Faith: A Workbook for Sponsors of Christian Initiation* by Thomas H. Morris.

A session held at the midpoint of the initiation process may offer sponsors a needed opportunity to share experiences and ideas.

There should also be a component of private formation for sponsors. Perhaps the practice of keeping a journal would be helpful. Each sponsor could record prayers, thoughts, and remembrances. If I were using this method, I would ask the sponsors to consider questions designed to stimulate their memories of their own experiences of God's grace and the roles of other people in assisting these experiences. It is hoped that such consideration would provide direction for sponsors as they seek to help form the initiates under their care.

If the goal is a guided reflection rather than a freer form of journaling, sponsors may use *Walking Together in Faith: A Workbook for Sponsors of Christian Initiation.* It includes several questions that prompt thought about the significance of crucial issues related to initiation, religious experience, and the ministry of sponsorship.

The third element in the formation and preparation of sponsors is a suggested reading list. A good place to begin is with the Christian Initiation series, particularly this handbook and *Come to the Waters: Baptism & Our Ministry of Welcoming Seekers & Making Disciples* by Daniel T. Benedict Jr. Since sponsors will work closely with catechists in the process of initiation, sponsors should read *Echoing the Word: The Ministry of Forming Disciples* by Grant Sperry-White. *Gracious Voices: Shouts & Whispers for God Seekers* by William P. McDonald is an anthology of thought-provoking passages about God's grace and call in baptism. This resouce can be a continuing source of inspiration for sponsors. If a congregation desires to provide additional exploration of the meaning of baptism in a group setting, *By Water and the Spirit: Making Connections for Identity and Ministry* by Gayle Felton is recommended. This book provides the text of the most recent baptism statement from General Conference, along with commentary and discussion suggestions.

PRAYER SUGGESTIONS FOR SPONSORS

Another helpful—indeed crucial—exercise for sponsors is active prayer for the initiate. Sponsors should pray regularly for their charges.

Perhaps the harder question is not *whether* to pray but *how* to pray. To pray regularly over an extended period of time for a single person is not necessarily an easy thing. Over a period of time, the petitions that were once filled with zeal can become stale. The greatest intercessory zeal can seem to deflate over time. And it takes time to properly form the initiate in the way of Christ.

But there are several ways to keep prayer for someone active and full of life. First, make sure you take time to be quiet, wait, listen, and observe. Praying does not always mean constant talking. Prayer can also include being still and silent. The benefits are numerous. Taking time for reflection makes you aware of how God has already answered your prayers for the initiate. Seeing that your prayers have been answered rejuvenates your prayer for the charge. Stillness in prayer often opens up new avenues or thoughts.

Second, use written sources of prayer to help expand your intercessory prayer. This does not necessarily mean that you merely repeat written prayers by memory. Rather, one can use the wisdom and the breadth of these prayers to stimulate new thought and direction in one's own praying. Of course, some of the prayers that will be suggested are worth praying word for word. Written prayers are like molds God can use. By praying them, one often finds that God has used the prayers to form her or him in a broader, more mature Christianity, resulting in fuller intercession.

Four suggestions are:

1. **Pray the Bible**. In particular, the opening prayers in the New Testament letters attributed to the apostle Paul are very helpful and instructive. Typically, Paul's letters begin with prayer concerns for the church receiving the letter. These prayers are vivid expressions of some of the deepest apostolic concerns for seeing Christians grow in grace; thus, they are helpful as prayers for modern-day Christians, including those who are preparing for baptism. Examples of these prayers include Romans 1:8-12, 1 Corinthians 1:4-9, Ephesians 1:15-23, Philippians 1:3-11, Colossians 1:3-14, 1 Thessalonians 1:2-7, 2 Thessalonians 1:3-4, and Philemon 4-7.

Use these biblical prayers in a variety of ways. Pray them directly and simply, if the prayer seems appropriate. The petitions in Colossians 1:9-10, for example, seem to be a ready-made prayer suitable for persons preparing for initiation: We pray that those so preparing "may be filled with the knowledge of God's will in all spiritual wisdom and understanding" so that they "may lead lives worthy of the Lord, fully pleasing to him," as they "bear fruit in every good work and…grow in the knowledge of God." Or, perhaps use the phrasing of the prayers for some reflective thought about the initiate's situation. The phrases in 2 Thessalonians 1:4 about "steadfastness and faith" during "persecutions and…afflictions" could prove fertile ground for thinking about the struggles of the one preparing for baptism and, thus, act as a stimulant to pray for these concerns. Take time to use these biblical prayers as a framework for your own specific intercessions.

2. **Pray the worship services**. Why should prayers used during worship be prayed over an initiate only once? Typically, these prayers strike at the crucial issues of being formed in Christ and in the Christian faith. They should be prayed repeatedly for the initiates. Sponsors should make sure they have a copy of the worship services (to be found in *The United Methodist Book of Worship* [pp. 81-114], *The United Methodist Hymnal* [pp. 33-54], and in *Come to the Waters* [pp. 99-150]). Read through the services. Find the prayers that will be prayed for the initiate, for you, for the congregation, and for others. Take time to pray them yourself, slowly and thoughtfully; feel free to supplement them with other intercessions. Do the same with other parts of the worship services. Take the part of the baptismal service, for instance, in which the initiate renounces evil and professes faith in Christ: Each phrase can be made into an intercession for God's grace to help the initiate live up to the pledges.

3. *Pray the* **Hymnal.** Particular phrases in hymns (or even the categories in which the hymns are organized) can prompt prayer ideas. The lyrics of the hymn "Breathe on Me, Breath of God" (*The United Methodist Hymnal*, No. 420) suggest possible points of intercession. Let those who are preparing for baptism be filled with "life anew," learning to love what God loves and learning to do what God would do. Even the hymn categories are useful in making sure your prayers on behalf of the initiate are sufficiently broad. For instance, the categories under the general heading of "The Power of the Holy Spirit" are helpful checkpoints for prayer. (See pages viii and ix in *The United Methodist Hymnal*.) Have we prayed for the initiate's repentance, pardon, sense of assurance before God, rebirth, personal holiness, social holiness, her or his own trust, hope, and strength in tribulation? Remembering the category of social holiness is especially helpful to me, for instance, since I admit (with shame) that I tend to forget this aspect of the gospel when I pray for others. Whatever omission you may tend toward, the use of these categories can help keep your intercessions broad and inclusive.

4. *Pray* **The Book of Worship.** There is much wealth in the prayers of others. *The Book of Worship* (see 497-530) has many of these prayers, and they can guide and shape your own prayers. The fruit of being guided by the prayers of others is that they also can help keep our intercessions broad and inclusive. Sometimes, when we have exhausted our own words or when our prayers seem to be running in the same well-worn ruts, the use of meaningful prayers first prayed by others can be helpful.

Do not forget to use these same resources to pray for yourself as sponsor, for catechists, and for other leaders involved in the process of Christian initiation. The importance of God's presence in those who are ministering to people preparing for initiation is manifestly obvious. Being filled with God's grace for these ministries is easier if one is surrounded in prayer. However, this is a truth that can be too easily forgotten in all the activity involved in the ministry. Part of the preparation and activity of sponsors and others involved in this important ministry is intercession for the leaders.

RESOURCES FOR SPONSORS

When considering resources for sponsors, begin by looking at the other volumes in the Christian Initiation series. These books are intended to be complementary volumes that introduce a clear process for evangelizing and forming adults preparing for baptism in The United Methodist Church. (See "Suggested Resources," pp. 79-80.)

The foundational volume in the series is *Come to the Waters: Baptism & Our Ministry of Welcoming Seekers & Making Disciples* by Daniel T. Benedict Jr. This book is divided into two parts. The first part describes basic ideas and understandings about the process of Christian initiation. The second part provides worship services and prayers for three kinds of situations: the initiation of adults never baptized, the initiation of children, and the initiation of returning persons (who have been previously baptized) to the baptismal covenant. The book provides the text and commentary for appropriate worship services in each case. Familiarity with this foundational volume is crucial for preparing well-informed sponsors. Every sponsor should own a copy and read it thoroughly. In fact, we strongly recommend that sponsors read *Come to the Waters* before or at the same time as they read *Accompanying the Journey*.

Another crucial volume in this series is *Gracious Voices: Shouts & Whispers for God Seekers*. This anthology, compiled and edited by William P. McDonald, is a useful and thought-provoking collection of quotes, prayers, meditations, and hymns, interwoven with Bible passages. The material is organized in a way to parallel the journey an initiate is making toward baptism. The book's goal is to provide resources for prayer, discussion, and reflection on the meaning of discipleship. It is useful not only for enriching the initiate's journey but also for enriching the spiritual lives of sponsors. Actual uses of the volume are many. It is highly recommended for use by sponsors, especially if it is read by initiates.

Two other volumes in this series are potentially helpful for sponsors. The first is *By Water and the Spirit: Making Connections for Identity and Ministry* by Gayle Felton. The heart of this book is the text of the study on baptism approved by the 1996 General Conference of The United Methodist Church. This baptismal study, entitled *By Water and the Spirit*, provides a Methodist history and understanding of baptism. Felton's volume provides a commentary on this study and guidance for group study over six sessions.

The last volume in this series, *Echoing the Word: The Ministry of Forming Disciples* by Grant Sperry-White is the handbook written to assist catechists (formation directors) in their ministry of forming initiates. This book can help sponsors understand how their role can supplement the vital ministry of catechists.

Beyond the volumes in the Christian Initiation series, several books have been written specifically to assist sponsors. Although they reflect Roman Catholic and Episcopalian perspectives, many of the insights can cross denominational lines and be useful for United Methodists. I have found the most helpful to be *Guide for Sponsors* by Ron Lewinski. Each chapter is concisely written, covering much important information. The chapters focus on some of the most important issues that face sponsors, including a basic definition of what it means to be a sponsor, the traits of an effective sponsor, a checklist for sponsors, and a discussion of common questions that sponsors have. In particular, the last chapter, entitled "A Sponsor's Time for Reflection and Prayer," lists Scriptures and insightful questions to help sponsors meditatively prepare for their important task.

Another book written to assist sponsors is *Finding and Forming Sponsors and Godparents*, edited by James A. Wilde. Many authors wrote the chapters in this book. This fact results in a little less continuity in thought. Nonetheless, some of the chapters are helpful and provocative. The chapter entitled, "Finding Sponsors and Godparents," for example, has some useful suggestions on selecting sponsors. The chapter entitled, "Adult Conversion and the Ministry of Sponsor," includes an interesting discussion on how the use of sponsors in the baptismal preparation of adults parallels the use of sponsors in Alcoholics Anonymous.

A third useful volume in this genre is *Walking Together in Faith: A Workbook for Sponsors of Christian Initiation* by Thomas H. Morris. This very helpful book truly lives up to its name: It is a *work*-book, with many reflective exercises designed to make sponsors more conscious of their ministry and spiritual journeys. The normal rhythm of this book is to provide a brief discussion of a topic followed by some written, reflective exercises. The book is very helpful for sponsors who desire an intense, involved preparation for their ministry.

For those who have been asked to serve as sponsors/godparents for small children, a helpful little book is *The Godparent Book: Ideas and Activities for Godparents and Their Godchildren* by Elaine Ramshaw. This book is mainly a series of short paragraphs, each describing practical things godparents can do to help raise their godchildren in the Christian faith. The suggestions are arranged by topics, including things to do at the time of baptism, ideas to make Sundays and the church year special, and book ideas for presents. *The Godparent Book* is written from a Roman Catholic perspective, yet many of its suggestions would be useful to other Christian denominations.

Two other books written from the same tradition also have brief, useful thoughts for sponsors. Both books fall toward the end of my recommended reading list, not because of their content but because the discussions of sponsors are relatively short. The usefulness of both books lies in their discussion of sponsors in the context of the other ministries involved in preparing people for baptism. The first of these books is *A Catechumenate Needs Everybody: Study Guides for Parish Ministers*, edited by James A. Wilde. The sheets in this book are perforated to allow for distribution to the leaders involved. The second of these books is *The Role of the Assembly in Christian Initiation* by Catherine Vincie. Because this book heavily addresses a Roman Catholic perspective on the roles of various ministries within a congregation's process of initiation, this book is not as helpful to United Methodists.

Similar short treatments of the role of sponsors can be found in books coming from other denominations. One extremely helpful book, though the chapter on sponsors is relatively short, is *The Catechumenal Process: Adult Initiation & Formation for Christian Life and Ministry*, produced by the Office of Evangelism Ministries of The Episcopal Church Center. Much of this work's discussion of sponsors is very helpful, condensing in a short space a basic "job description" for sponsors and key issues in selecting sponsors.

Another work from the same tradition is *Making Disciples: Serving Those Who Are Entering the Christian Life* by John W. B. Hill, a clergyperson in the Anglican Church of Canada. The most helpful insight of this work is Hill's insistence that inquirers should not select their own sponsors. His reasoning shows genuine pastoral experience.

Some of these latter books highlight other resources that could be helpful for sponsors. These resources provide a general description of the process of Christian initiation. Sometimes these books make only the briefest reference to sponsors but, nonetheless, they can provide an outline of the process that is helpful for everyone involved. There are several written from a Protestant point of view.

One easy-to-read resource, totally dedicated to explaining the recovery of Christian initiation, is *Liturgical Evangelism: Worship as Outreach and Nurture* by Robert E. Webber. The expressed purpose of this book is to advocate restoring the structures and patterns of the early church as a viable means of relating evangelism and worship in our times.

Readers who want a condensed explanation of a restored catechumenate as a model for initiation should look at the articles in Chapter Thirteen of *The Ministries of Christian Worship*, vol. 7, of *The Complete Library of Christian Worship*, edited by Robert E. Webber. Although the articles concentrate on the Roman Catholic adaptation of Christian initiation, called the Rite of Christian Initiation of Adults (RCIA), they are presented in a way that can give Protestants insight into the process of initiation. The articles on the RCIA are followed by others that provide a broader background to the issue of relating worship and evangelism.

An interesting, brief discussion of the role that a restored catechumenate can play in the modern church is found in *The Witness of the Worshiping Community: Liturgy and the Practice of Evangelism* by Frank C. Senn. Notice particularly the last two chapters. This discussion is especially useful because Senn, a Lutheran pastor, attempts to present a catechumenal initiation process as a more viable alternative to "church growth" methods of making new Christians.

Another Lutheran discussion of the catechumenate is provided in *Welcoming the Stranger: A Public Theology of Worship and Evangelism* by Patrick R. Keifert. Desiring a more sophisticated theological discussion, Keifert locates his understanding of the catechumenate under a broad metaphor of the church's hospitality to strangers.

A helpful book is *Models of Confirmation and Baptismal Affirmation: Liturgical and Educational Issues and Designs* by Robert L. Browning and Roy A. Reed. As the title suggests, the authors wish to give an overview of the different ways they have found confirmation and baptismal affirmation are handled in a variety of churches. Many of their comments are useful for looking at the educational issues involved in initiation and for suggesting ways to use sponsors.

Finally, one other resource may be useful for sponsors to gain insight in their role of forming new Christians: reviewing the classic Methodist position of class leader. In early Methodism a class leader was the person who provided encouragement and accountability as Methodists sought to grow in grace and the knowledge of God. Studying the historic role of the class leader may help a sponsor discover how ordinary Methodists of the past provided encouragement, accountability, nourishment, and guidance for progressing as a Christian—the role that sponsors play. Two recent books by David Lowes Watson may be helpful for a United Methodist perspective on this role: *Class Leaders: Recovering a Tradition* and Chapter Nine in *Forming Christian Disciples: The Role of Covenant Discipleship and Class Leaders in the Congregation*.

QUESTIONS FOR REFLECTION

❧ Which do you think is the more desirable characteristic in sponsors: a degree of detachment to provide a sense of objectivity in assessing the initiate's progress in grace or a degree of closeness to create a real bond in the relationship? Are the two mutually exclusive?

❧ What do you think is the best method for selecting sponsors? Why?

❧ Do you agree with the sentiment in this book that it is best for family members not to serve as sponsors for a relative? Why or why not?

❧ Are there additional qualities desirable in a sponsor that are not listed above? Why do you think the qualities you added to the list are important?

❧ How do you think a process of Christian initiation could become a formative experience for sponsors and catechists—even the whole church—and not just those preparing for baptism and initiation?

❧ Could prayer itself be considered the foremost expression of the church's concern for the newly baptized and the newly received? What special role do you think sponsors should have in praying for those preparing for baptism?

Chapter Six

A BRIEF HISTORY OF THE ROLE OF A SPONSOR

SPONSORS IN THE EARLY CHURCH

The position of sponsor is a venerable one, dating back to the earliest periods of church history. If you are serving as a sponsor today, you are part of a long train of faithful Christians who have served God and built up the church. The work of sponsors has been—and remains—a vital one as new members must be fully received into the life of the congregation and trained in the way of Christ.

Historical data records the role of sponsor as important in initiating new members. But sketching a full picture of the sponsor's role in the early church is more difficult because of scant information. What is available for the most part are brief references—isolated "snapshots," if you will—about sponsors. Although not a complete picture, these snapshots, when put together, tell us something about sponsors in the early church, particularly their importance in preparing people for baptism. These snapshots also demonstrate that the role of sponsor in the early church was not unlike that described in this book. Let us take a look at a few of these portrayals of early sponsors to see the similarity.

One important source is a document generally known as *The Apostolic Tradition*, whose descriptions of worship might reflect practices as early as the beginning of the third century. Two references are made to a kind of baptismal sponsor in *The Apostolic Tradition*. In both cases, the reference is to a sponsor (although this title itself is not used) providing witness for adults who have come to the church to hear the gospel and to be baptized. The first reference is a description of the initial approach by inquirers: "And let them be examined as to the reason why they have come forward to the faith. And those who bring them shall bear witness for them whether they are able to hear."[28]

Here we see sponsors fulfilling one of their most crucial roles: presenting inquirers to the church by attesting to their ability to hear the gospel in a significant way. The broader context of this document shows some of that era's concerns about the inquirers' abilities to hear the gospel. Given the situation of the church in those ancient times, certain professions and activities were deemed contrary to the values of the gospel. Thus, sponsors were probably called upon to witness that inquirers were not so entangled with something contrary to Christianity that they were unable to hear the Word effectually.

That this effectual hearing of the gospel, evidenced by a life now led in visible Christian service, was the goal of inquirers' formation is clear from the other passage about sponsors in *The Apostolic Tradition*. After a period of formative instruction, the inquirers' lives would be re-examined. The investigation had a very practical bent to it. Those preparing for baptism were examined as to "whether they lived piously..., whether they 'honoured the widows,' whether they visited the sick, [and] whether they have fulfilled every good work."[29] And who did the church ask to attest to this type of formation? Again, it is the sponsors who provided the witness that triggered the inquirers' intensive preparation for baptism.

Notice also the implied role of accompaniment by these sponsors in *The Apostolic Tradition*. Indeed the name "sponsor" is not even used; they are more generally identified by action. In this document, sponsors were known by what they did: They were "those who bring" the inquirers.

Accounts from later in the early church likewise emphasize familiar duties of sponsors, including accompanying candidates during worship and attesting to their character and growth in faith. One particularly interesting account was written by a woman on a pilgrimage to Jerusalem in the late fourth century. Part of the description by this woman—known as Egeria or Etheria—includes a description of how adults were prepared for baptism in that city. Egeria's description features an eight-week period of Lent. Preparation began on the first day of Lent at a service in a church called the Martyrium, built on what was thought to be Golgotha. It was a solemn sight. The bishop sat on a throne, surrounded by a multitude of priests and other clergy. One by one the candidates for baptism were led in, not surprisingly—as Egeria notes—accompanied by their sponsors. Egeria also says that these sponsors were called godfathers or godmothers and that sponsors were the same gender as their candidates. Then the bishop questioned those who knew each candidate as to his or her manner of life:

> Then the candidates are brought in one by one, the men with their "fathers," the women with their "mothers." Then the bishop one by one asks their neighbours: "Is he a good-living man? Does he respect his parents? Is he a drunkard or untrustworthy?" He asks them like this about every vice, at least the more serious ones.[30]

Although Egeria does not mention the sponsors themselves witnessing to the faith of the candidates, that role would have been natural for them at this point. Finally, Egeria describes how the sponsors accompanied their candidates on each day of Lent as the bishop taught the meaning of the Christian faith to the candidates.

The importance of a sponsor witnessing on behalf of his or her candidate was crucial during the period of early church history, as shown by another late fourth-century writer. John Chrysostom was a priest in the church at Antioch in Syria. There, he preached a series of sermons to those preparing for baptism. During one of these sermons, Chrysostom paused to address the sponsors who accompanied their candidates. Because this address is one of the few extended passages from the early church about sponsors and because the passage highlights some of sponsors' classic roles, it will be reproduced here in full. Chrysostom's basic image is that of a sponsor as a kind of co-signer on a note or loan:

> Do you wish me to address a word to those who are sponsoring you, that they too may know what recompense they deserve if they have shown great care for you, and what condemnation follows if they are careless? Consider, beloved, how those who go surety for someone in a matter of money set up for themselves a greater risk than the one who borrows the money and is liable for it. If the borrower be well disposed, he lightens the burden for his surety; if the dispositions of his soul be ill, he makes the risk a steeper one. Wherefore, the wise man counsels us, saying: *If thou be surety, think as if thou wert to pay it.* If, then, those who go surety for others in a matter of money make themselves liable for the whole sum, those who go surety for others in matters of the spirit and on an account which involves virtue should be much more alert. They ought to show their paternal love by encouraging, counseling, and correcting those for whom they go surety.
>
> Let them not think that what takes place is a trifling thing, but let them see clearly that they share in the credit if by their admonition they lead those entrusted to them to the path of virtue. Again, if those they sponsor become careless, the sponsors themselves will suffer great punishment. That is why it is customary to call the sponsors "spiritual fathers," that they may learn by this very action how great an affection they must show to those they sponsor in the matter of spiritual instruction. If it is a noble thing to lead to a zeal for virtue those who are in no way related to us, much more should we fulfill this precept in the case of the one whom we receive as a spiritual son. You, the sponsors, have learned that no slight danger hangs over your heads if you are remiss.[31]

The intensity of Chrysostom's rhetoric underscores how much his ancient church truly relied upon the testimony of sponsors concerning the Christian character and faith of their candidates and their readiness for baptism. According to Chrysostom, a sponsor "co-signs" on the reliability of the candidate's faith. The affirmation of faith that a candidate makes at the time of baptism follows the sponsor's witness on a candidate's behalf. Chrysostom wants sponsors in his church to feel as if they will be held liable if their respective candidates "default" on the faith. Thus, he wants them to take seriously their roles of "encouraging, counseling, and correcting." Here we see the point of connection between presenting a candidate to the church (the witness to the candidate's faith and character) and presenting the church to a candidate (the encouragement, counsel, and accountability).

Note that this passage from Chrysostom also highlights some of the other classic roles of sponsors. Chrysostom insists that sponsors take seriously their job of giving "spiritual instruction," leading to a cultivation of a "zeal for virtue." Interestingly he ties this idea of instruction to that of being a spiritual "parent" for the candidate. Finally, notice that the sponsors apparently accompanied candidates in special services, evidenced by the fact that Chrysostom was able to stop in the middle of a sermon to baptismal candidates and speak to their sponsors.

Accompaniment and witness were not the only presentation roles of sponsors in the early church. In some churches, at least, sponsors presented objects to their candidates. For example, at another church in Syria in the early fifth century, the renouncing of Satan and the powers of evil took place in a vivid ceremony in which sponsors played an important role. As described by a bishop named Theodore, the renunciation was made as the candidates were kneeling. Then, the bishop anointed each candidate's forehead with oil. Finally, the sponsor, who had been standing behind his or her candidate, placed a linen stole over the candidate's head and raised him or her to a standing position. At the time, this ceremony had great significance: Because only nonslaves could wear these stoles, the sponsor's act represented that the candidate had passed from slavery in sin to freedom in Christ.[32]

Theodore's preaching is also helpful in providing an insightful image for sponsors. At one point Theodore describes the church as a city and a sponsor as a guide to the city. The sponsor uses prior familiarity with the church and Christianity to help the newcomer navigate. How much easier it is to avoid getting lost if one has a good guide. So it is with a sponsor: He or she should help the newly baptized gain familiarity with and direction in the church.

The role of sponsor as guide was also emphasized by another fifth century Syrian Christian. A work entitled *Ecclesiastical Hierarchy*, whose precise author is unknown, described how those seeking baptism had to take the first step to find someone who was already baptized as a member of the church to serve as a guide for admission to the bishop.[33] Sponsors were the bridge for the initial contacts between inquirers and the church. Not surprisingly, when the candidate's name was recorded as one preparing for baptism, his or her sponsor's name was recorded too. (This practice was also done elsewhere.)

This work also reveals something about some sponsors' willingness—or unwillingness—to assume this responsibility. The author notes that a realization of their task's importance and a sense of inadequacy often left sponsors fearful. The author further observes, however, that a sense of calling could overcome this anxiety and help sponsors move beyond their hesitancy.

Ecclesiastical Hierarchy also describes the sponsors making physical presentations. According to this work, after initiates were baptized, their sponsors assisted in clothing them in new garments appropriate to their new status.

SPONSORS IN THE MIDDLE AGES

In some ways the role of sponsor in the medieval period maintained some lines of continuity with the early church. However, because of some significant shifts in the practice of baptism itself, the role of sponsor underwent some fundamental changes too.

Perhaps the most central shift in baptismal practice, as the church moved into the medieval period, was the utter predominance of infant baptism across all of Christianity. For the most part, baptism of adults who could profess faith on their own became an extremely unfamiliar practice, except in missionary situations and other circumstances.

The fact that infant baptism became the norm also affected certain aspects of the timing of baptism. The most fundamental change was a shortening of the time between birth and baptism. For a variety of reasons, the vast majority of children were presented for baptism shortly after birth. This shortening of time was accompanied by three other changes. One was that the timing of baptism became much less connected to the rhythms of the church's calendar and much more connected to family rhythms. Another change was the gradual absorption of pre-baptismal services into the baptismal service itself. With no extended period of pre-baptismal formation, there was no need for worship services to mark the thresholds of preparation. Thus, in the third change, the standard period of Christian formation was assumed to take place after baptism and was much less connected to formal structures or programs.[34]

What this meant for baptismal sponsors is that, even if certain basic actions of sponsors (or godparents, the more common term of the time) did not change, the context for initiation was much different than that in the early church. The change in context affected the role of the sponsor. Perhaps, in some ways, there was less change in the sponsor's activities within the baptismal rite itself. Many of the basic acts of presentation remained stable for centuries: holding the infant, naming him or her, receiving the child from the baptismal font, and marking him or her with the sign of the cross in some instances.

One crucial role a sponsor played in the service of baptism was to answer all questions on behalf of the infant, including the renunciation of evil and the confession of faith in Christ. Not surprisingly, some commentators at the time really emphasized the notion of sponsors as sureties, or guarantors, of the infants' faith since sponsors were not just attesting that their adult charges had faith—as in the early period of the church—but were actually expressing faith on behalf of their infant charges.

The baptismal services used in different locations varied as to whether a sponsor alone spoke for an infant or whether a sponsor and parents together answered. This difference in practice reflects an ambivalence inherent in infant baptism about who most naturally should be the sponsor for a baptized child: the parents or a representative of the church. Indeed, some scholars are convinced that historically non-parental sponsors were first used only with orphans, but eventually the practice of having sponsors for all infants dominated, displacing the natural role of parents.[35]

Outside the sponsorial role in the baptismal service itself, the changed context for baptism greatly affected the role of sponsors in the formation of their charges. While sponsors were still held responsible for forming their charges in the Christian faith, there was no specific time of preparation or formation. Thus, the responsibility seems to have been a more general one, following baptism. When instruction of their charges was mentioned, sponsors were usually told to make sure they taught the Lord's Prayer, the Creed, and the Hail Mary, as well as general Christian virtue. Many sponsors were also frequently encouraged to make sure their charges received the rite of confirmation when it became available. (Note that in the medieval period confirmation was not seen as a period of education or training.)

SPONSORS AMONG EARLY PROTESTANTS

As Protestantism emerged in the sixteenth century and different Protestant groups altered the baptismal service, the role of sponsors remained relatively unchanged, at least initially. For most Protestants, the practice of infant baptism still predominated.

(Groups called Anabaptists were the major exceptions.) Thus, most Protestant baptismal services—like the medieval services from which they emerged—called for sponsors/godparents to be as active as parents, or more. Typically, sponsors continued to answer the questions about renouncing evil and professing faith in Christ on behalf of their infant charges. If anything, Protestant leaders encouraged sponsors to be even more responsible for teaching after baptism the faith professed at baptism. This emphasis on teaching reflected general Protestant sensibilities of the time.

Under Protestant influence some changes did occur in the role of sponsors. For example, *generally* Protestants tended to prune the number of ceremonial actions in worship services. Thus, as some Protestants continued to revise the baptismal services that they had inherited, a good chance existed that sponsors' responsibilities during worship services were reduced. This tendency resulted in emphasizing sponsors' accompaniment and speaking roles in worship. And even the latter came under review by some Protestants. Specifically, some Protestant leaders grew uncomfortable with the idea of sponsors speaking on behalf of infants; they argued that sponsors can speak only for themselves and the questions posed to sponsors in the service should be seen as pledges by sponsors to teach the faith at the appropriate time.[36] Even if the actual form of the questions was not changed, it can be assumed that under such a viewpoint the addresses to sponsors took on a more exhortatory flavor.

SPONSORS IN METHODISM

The role of baptismal sponsors among American Methodists has been hard to ascertain until recently. The place to begin is with the work of John Wesley, one of the founders of the Methodist movement. But Wesley's attitude is hard to pin down. Although toward the beginning of his ministry he wrote a treatise discussing favorably and with much zeal the usefulness of the position of sponsor, by the end of his ministry his thought is much less clear. In 1784, for instance, when Wesley developed a book of worship services for American Methodists by revising the *Book of Common Prayer* of the Church of England, he eliminated all specific mention of sponsors (or godparents) from the baptismal services. All that remained was for "friends of the child" (Wesley's phrase) to answer the question about the name of the child-to-be-baptized.[37]

Officially, within the texts of the baptismal services, this lack of reference to sponsors remained until the twentieth century. Of course, it is much more difficult to ascertain what may have been taking place unofficially. Laypeople, clergy, and congregations sometimes go beyond what is described or allowed in the official worship texts. Practices seen in other denominations and viewed as useful are easily appropriated even if there is no official sanction. And, thus, it is possible that a constant practice of using godparents in the baptism of children continued in Methodism.

If so, that could help explain the increasing recurrence of the term "sponsor" in the worship services of twentieth-century Methodism. The first specific reference came in the Methodist Episcopal Church's 1916 revision of the baptismal service for infants. The instructions of this service noted that not only parents but "other sponsors" were called upon to pledge to bring the child up in the Christian faith and to name the child. The comparable service at the time for the Methodist Episcopal Church, South, did not include any such provision. However, after these two denominations cooperated on a hymnal in the 1930's and after they merged in 1939, not only the infant baptismal service but also the service for receiving children and youth into the church included references to "sponsors" and parents. In like manner, the *Book of Worship* published in the mid-1960's by the Methodist Church—the denomination resulting from the 1939 merger of the Methodist Episcopal Church, the Methodist Episcopal Church, South, and the Methodist Protestant Church—included a role for sponsors in the baptism of infants. Along with parents, sponsors could confess faith, pledge to bring up the child as a Christian, and give the name of the child when asked. Of course, as noted previously, actual practice is harder to determine. It is possible that these provisions were used as opportunities for families to select godparents for sentimental reasons.

Several things should be noted about the way the texts for Methodist baptismal services mentioned sponsors until recently because the references contrast with the way sponsors have been presented in this book and its companion volumes. First, previously the services only mentioned sponsors in the case of the baptism of infants or small children. In no case in which the one being baptized answered for himself or herself was there ever a provision for a sponsor. The second is related: Any pledge to assist the one being baptized—presumed to be a child—extends beyond baptism since actual formation in the faith can only be done after baptism. The services also did not presume that sponsors would assist in the formation of parents before the baptism of their child. Simply put, if sponsors were used in Methodism previously, their role was limited to participating in the baptismal service for infants and to assisting in the subsequent formation of the child in the Christian faith.

RECENT DEVELOPMENTS IN SPONSORSHIP

If the role of sponsors described in this book is significantly different from the role previously assumed in Methodist services, from where did the difference come? The answer stems from a growing awareness of the early church's understanding of the nature of baptism and of its practice of baptismal preparation. Many passages in the first part of this chapter—and related material from the early history of the church—have become increasingly influential among United Methodist and other scholars in the last thirty years or so.

Seeing the value in the early church's way of doing things concerning baptism, many churches have sought to appropriate some of these insights. Thus, it is common for sponsors to have a prominent role in a developed structure to evangelize people, prepare them for baptism, and assist in their integration into the church's life and ministry. This same basic idea has found an increasing place in denominations from Methodist to Roman Catholic, not to mention other Protestant denominations. These churches have developed an increasing amount of literature on the baptismal process, including the role of sponsors.

This renewed emphasis on sponsors results from several basic shifts concerning baptism in general. Foremost is a renewed emphasis on the baptism of adults as a central aspect of the church's life. Thus, the concern about sponsors is not a description of their role in the baptism of children, but of adults. Any role in children's baptism is a derived one. Likewise, by a renewed emphasis on evangelizing and baptizing adults, the church becomes focused on the manner in which adults are properly introduced and formed in the faith prior to baptism. Thus, the idea of a sponsor as someone who accompanies and assists before baptism becomes a key concern. (The awareness that this sort of formation ought to be intentional for adults who have not been fully integrated is the idea behind using sponsors for other kinds of adult initiates.) Finally, a shift is usually seen in a renewed emphasis on parents as the primary sponsors when children are baptized. In this situation, sponsors function to exert a kind of formative influence on the parents.

If you are a sponsor, realize that you are not only helping to introduce a person into the church's life but also that you are part of the vanguard as God does something new in the church today. Your position as a sponsor is a venerable one. It is also an occasion for God's renewal of the church today. May God use your faithfulness for the benefit of all concerned.

QUESTIONS FOR REFLECTION

⚐ Of the different "snapshots" presented in this chapter, which did you find the most helpful to your role as sponsor? Which was the most inspiring? Which was the least helpful? Why?

⚐ What surprised you about the role of sponsors in previous periods of church history?

⚐ Would it be fair to say that it has been a balancing act to relate the role of parents presenting their children for baptism and the role of the sponsors of these children? How would you describe the way these roles should be related?

⚐ Why are scholars and churches studying and adapting early church models for modern structures of baptism preparation? What advantages or disadvantages does looking at the early church, as compared to other periods of church history, have?

Appendix

An Order for Commissioning Sponsors

The sponsor's task of accompanying an initiate in the journey toward baptism and, subsequently, in the new member's integration into the community of faith is an awesome one. It is also a task that ultimately belongs to the whole congregation. Setting aside a time to commission sponsors for this important venture stresses the joy, resolve, and responsibility on the part of both the sponsors and the congregation as they engage in the process of Christian initiation.

The Order for Commissioning Sponsors outlined below may be used at any time when persons are being set apart to serve as sponsors. While it is written with several sponsors in view, changes can easily be made to address one sponsor.

As a Response to the Word or at some other appropriate place within a public worship service, the pastor invites the persons undertaking the ministry of sponsor to come forward. The pastor says to the congregation:

Dear friends, standing before us today are *those* who will represent us to persons seeking to know Christ and learn his way. Let us hear *their* pledge to fulfill faithfully this ministry, as God grants help and grace.

The pastor says to the sponsors:
By your companionship, will you accompany those who are preparing for initiation into Christ's church?

I will.

By your constant concern, will you extend the care, love, support, and encouragement to them that God shows through the church?

I will.

By your example, will you present to them the treasures with which God has graced the church: its faith, its worship, its service, and its fellowship?

I will.

By your witness, will you testify truthfully concerning those preparing for Christian initiation?

I will.

The pastor says to the congregation:
You have heard the pledge of *these sponsors* to accept this solemn ministry. As the church, the body of Christ, will you support *these sponsors,* accepting *them* as your *representatives,* and will you do all that is within you power to live as a fellowship redeemed by God for the sake of those who wish to join us?

We will.

The pastor prays:
Almighty and loving God, you have promised to reveal your saving glory through your Son, Jesus Christ. Pour out your Holy Spirit upon us, and especially upon *these sponsors* so that your church may be a people through whom others come to know Christ Jesus and learn to follow his way. We pray through Christ, our Lord. Amen.

The sponsors take their seats. If the order of commissioning was used as a Response to the Word, the worship continues with the Concerns and Prayers.

ENDNOTES

1 John Wesley, "Upon our Lord's Sermon on the Mount, Discourse IV," in *Sermons on Several Occasions* (London: Epworth Press, 1944), p. 237.

2 Daniel T. Benedict Jr., *Come to the Waters: Baptism & Our Ministry of Welcoming Seekers & Making Disciples* (Nashville: Discipleship Resources, 1996), p. 55.

3 See Michel Dujarier, *A History of the Catechumenate*, trans. Edward J. Haasl (New York: Sadlier), pp. 45, 56, 110.

4 Benedict, *Come to the Waters*, pp. 22-23.

5 *The United Methodist Hymnal* (Nashville: The United Methodist Publishing House, 1989), p. 35.

6 Ebenezer Francis Newell, *Life and Observations of Rev. E. F. Newell* (Worcester, MA: C. W. Ainsworth, 1847), pp. 37-38.

7 William Harmless, S.J., *Augustine and the Catechumenate* (Collegeville, MN: The Liturgical Press, 1995), p. 10.

8 Aidan Kavanagh, *The Shape of Baptism: The Rite of Christian Initiation* (New York: Pueblo Publishing Company, 1978), p. 131.

9 John Wesley, "A Plain Account of the People called Methodists," in *The Methodist Societies*, vol. 9 of *The Works of John Wesley*, ed. Rupert E. Davies (Nashville: Abingdon Press, 1989), p. 258.

10 Benedict, *Come to the Waters*, p. 16.

11 For instructions and an explanation of these practices, see the baptismal services in *The United Methodist Book of Worship* (Nashville: The United Methodist Publishing House, 1992), pp. 91 and 98.

12 Benedict, *Come to the Waters*, p. 138.

13 Ibid., p. 147.

14 William Keith, *The Experience of William Keith. [Written by Himself.] Together with Some Observations Conclusive of Divine Influence on the Mind of Man* (Utica: Seward, 1806).

15 Paul D. Stanley and J. Robert Clinton, *Connecting: The Mentoring Relationships You Need to Succeed in Life* (Copyright © 1992). Used by permission of NavPress, p. 124. For copies call 1-800-366-7788.

16 Ibid., p. 125.

17 Benedict, *Come to the Waters*, p. 109.

18 Ibid., p. 153.

19 Ibid., pp. 113-114.

20 Ibid., p. 113.

21 Ibid., p. 153.

22 Cynthia Zirlott, electronic correspondence, 21 March 1997; Zirlott's work in this area is based upon Adrian van Kaam's *Fundamental Formation* (New York: Crossroads, 1989), p. 231ff especially.

23 Benedict, *Come to the Waters*, pp. 106-107.

24 Ibid., p. 134.

25 James A. Wilde, "Finding Sponsors and Godparents" in *Finding and Forming Sponsors and Godparents* (Chicago: Liturgy Training Publications, 1988), pp. 20-21.

26 Office of Evangelism Ministries of the Episcopal Church, *The Catechumenal Process* (New York: The Church Hymnal Corporation, 1990), p. 103. Reprinted by permission of the Domestic and Foreign Missionary Society of the Protestant Episcopal Church USA.

27 Leroy Lee, *The Life and Times of The Rev. Jesse Lee* (Richmond, VA: John Early, 1848), p. 69.

28 Gregory Dix and Henry Chadwick, eds., *The Treatise on the Apostolic Tradition of St. Hippolytus of Rome.* Copyright © 1991 Elmore Abbey, first published 1937; Second revised edition 1968, reissued 1992. Used with permission of Morehouse Publishing, p. 23.

29 Ibid., pp. 30-31.

30 See Edward Yarnold, *The Awe-Inspiring Rites of Initiation.* Copyright © by the Order of St. Benedict, Inc. Published by The Liturgical Press, Collegeville, MN. Used with permission, pp. 8-9.

31 Paul W. Harkins, trans., *St. John Chrysostom: Baptismal Instructions* (New York: Newman Press, 1963), pp. 48-49. Reprinted from ANCIENT CHRISTIAN WRITERS by Paul W. Harkins, Ph.D., LL.D. Copyright © 1963 by Rev. Johannes Quasten & Rev. Walter J. Burghardt, S.J. Used by permission of Paulist Press.

32 See Yarnold, *The Awe-Inspiring Rites of Initiation*, p. 179.

33 See Colm Luibheid, trans., *Pseudo-Dionysius: The Complete Works* (New York: Paulist Press, 1987), pp. 201-203.

34 This sketch is just a summary of changes that took centuries to evolve. For a much fuller discussion of this history, see J. D. C. Fisher, *Christian Initiation: Baptism in the Medieval West*, Alcuin Club Collection No. XLVII (London: S.P.C.K., 1965), pp. 101-120.

35 Michel Dujarier, "Sponsorship" in *Adult Baptism and the Catechumenate*, Concilium vol. 22 (New York: Paulist Press, 1967), p. 47.

36 See, for example, J. D. C. Fisher, *Christian Initiation: The Reformation Period*, Alcuin Club Collections No. 51 (London: S.P.C.K., 1970), p. 103.

37 For a fuller discussion, see Gayle Carlton Felton, *This Gift of Water: The Practice and Theology of Baptism Among Methodists in America* (Nashville: Abingdon Press, 1992), p. 22.

Suggested Resources

Benedict, Daniel T. Jr. *Come to the Waters: Baptism & Our Ministry of Welcoming Seekers & Making Disciples.* Nashville: Discipleship Resources, 1996.

Browning, Robert L. and Roy A. Reed. *Models of Confirmation and Baptismal Affirmation: Liturgical and Educational Issues and Designs.* Birmingham: Religious Education Press, 1995.

Felton, Gayle. *By Water and the Spirit: Making Connections for Identity and Ministry.* Nashville: Discipleship Resources, 1997.

Guthrie, Clifton F., ed. *For All the Saints: A Calendar of Commemorations for United Methodists.* Akron, OH: Order of Saint Luke Publications, 1995.

Hill, John W. B. *Making Disciples: Serving Those Who Are Entering the Christian Life.* Toronto: The Hoskin Group, 1991.

Keifert, Patrick R. *Welcoming the Stranger: A Public Theology of Worship and Evangelism.* Minneapolis: Fortress Press, 1992.

Lewinski, Ron. *Guide for Sponsors.* Chicago: Liturgy Training Publications, 1993.

McDonald, William P., ed. *Gracious Voices: Shouts & Whispers for God Seekers.* Nashville: Discipleship Resources, 1996.

Morris, Thomas H. *Walking Together in Faith: A Workbook for Sponsors of Christian Initiation.* New York: Paulist Press, 1992.

Office of Evangelism Ministries of The Episcopal Church Center. *The Catechumenal Process: Adult Initiation & Formation for Christian Life and Ministry.* New York: The Church Hymnal Corporation, 1990.

Ramshaw, Elaine. *The Godparent Book: Ideas and Activities for Godparents and Their Godchildren.* Chicago: Liturgy Training Publications, 1993.

Senn, Frank C. *The Witness of the Worshiping Community: Liturgy and the Practice of Evangelism.* New York: Paulist Press, 1993.

Sperry-White, Grant S. *Echoing the Word: The Ministry of Forming Disciples.* Nashville: Discipleship Resources, 1998.

The United Methodist Book of Worship. Nashville: United Methodist Publishing House, 1992.

The United Methodist Hymnal. Nashville: United Methodist Publishing House, 1989.

Vincie, Catherine. *The Role of the Assembly in Christian Initiation.* Chicago: Liturgy Training Publications, 1993.

Watson, David Lowes. *Class Leaders: Recovering a Tradition.* Nashville: Discipleship Resources, 1991.

————. *Forming Christian Disciples: The Role of Covenant Discipleship and Class Leaders in the Congregation.* Nashville: Discipleship Resources, 1991.

Webber, Robert E. *Liturgical Evangelism: Worship as Outreach and Nurture.* Harrisburg, PA: Morehouse Publishing, 1986.

Webber, Robert E., ed. *The Complete Library of Christian Worship,* vol. 7. Nashville: Star Song Publishing Group, 1994.

Wilde, James A., ed. *A Catechumenate Needs Everybody: Study Guides for Parish Ministers.* Chicago: Liturgy Training Publications, 1988.

————. *Finding and Forming Sponsors and Godparents.* Chicago: Liturgy Training Publications, 1988.